Pity my simplicity

PITY MY SIMPLICITY

A confession in defence of the simple truth
that has been complicated in our age

John Wilson

 EVANGELICAL PRESS

EVANGELICAL PRESS
P.O. Box 5, Welwyn, Hertfordshire AL6 9NU, England.

© Evangelical Press 1980.
First published 1980

ISBN 0 85234 140 7

Cover design by Peter Wagstaff

Typeset in 11 on 12 pt Baskerville by Beaver Publishing Services Ltd.,
Maidstone, Kent.
Printed in Great Britain by The Pitman Press, Bath.

To

JEAN

who shares my simple faith
and especially because we share
all things together.

Contents

Prologue
An introductory bleat

Although he is a lay preacher and occasionally in the pulpit, the proper place for this particular sheep is in the pew and, truth to tell, he is happiest there. There is great comfort to be found in simply being one of the flock of God. But even sheep know something of the best grazing places, can appreciate good food, and are entitled to have an opinion on shepherds and veterinary surgeons.

So this bleat of a book is really something of a confession of faith; it is personal, simple, even occasionally satirical, but it is not naive. It is an honest attempt to explain why he cannot follow those clever shepherds who would lead him into the concrete paths and plastic pastures of what passes for 'modern theology'. Of course, as a mere sheep, he is unqualified to give detailed critiques of particular theological systems or schools of philosophical thought; it is goats that are made for climbing, and surely it is too much to expect a simple sheep to scale the dizzy heights of higher criticism. So, in his simplicity, he may be accused of lumping together, without naming them, the thoughts of such reverent names as Bultmann and Barth, Brunner and Bonhoeffer, Tillich and Moltmann, de Chardin and Pannenberg, and the other learned shepherds of our age whose names are legion. But what really concerns this sheep is not any one theologian or system, it is the whole ethos of liberalism and modernism which has permeated colleges, universities, religious magazines and books, and even the pulpits of almost all the folds where the sheep gather.

This sheep confesses that he is without formal training in

theology but suspects that this may be a valuable asset. He
has not been herded about by yapping young radicals or
driven in endless circles by intellectual whiz-shepherds; he has
had to find his own way through the thorns and thickets of
modern thought. It also means he knows something of
modern liberal theology from the viewpoint of the recipient.
He has learned it from books and papers, from pew and
lecture hall, and not from the rarified atmosphere of the
Shepherd Common Room where wolves, cliffs and quick-
sands must seem academic concepts rather than an ever-
present danger and possibility.

It must be confessed that he knows that much of what he
will say will be dismissed with an impatient wave of the
crook — sadly even shepherds can be arrogant. Doubtless he
will be accused of being an unthinking fundamentalist, and it
is not simply pride that makes him want to dispute the adjec-
tive and be unhappy at the connotations of the noun. Worse
than that, he will be treated as an extreme literalist, and this
will hurt his sheepish pride by making him appear to be
totally ignorant of grammatical structure and literary forms.
Such an accusation will imply that when he reads the words
of Jesus, 'I am the door,' he immediately assumes that the
Saviour of men is a flat piece of wood measuring something
like seven feet by three feet six inches. But he is not as sheep-
ishly stupid as all that; even sheep are not necessarily woolly
thinkers.

Simply stated, his position is that of a simple sheep who
simply believes the Bible. He believes that God has spoken to
men in a written revelation and His word is true — not simply
mythologically, existentially, experientially, philosophically
or poetically true — but in the plain meaning of the word. He
accepts his Bible as being true in the way his Concise Oxford
Dictionary defines the word: 'being in accordance with fact
or reality. . . in accordance with reason. . . genuine, not
spurious or hybrid or counterfeit or merely apparent, having
all the attributes implied in the name'.

To many modern scholarly shepherds, such a confession
will mean that he should be confined to a Sheepiatric Ward.

He will be beaten with the staff of 'The battles were fought long ago' and without the benefit of a veterinary anaesthetic the unpalatable medicine of 'the assured results of modern scholarship' will be forced down his throat. Perhaps it is because sheep have myopic eyes, but he sees no reason why the past should be ignored and theology should be treated as if it began in the late nineteenth century. If the philosophers of ancient Athens are still relevant today, then it seems to him that the writers of the Bible should be given the same courtesy. Then this poor little sheep often finds himself wondering if the 'assured results of modern scholarship' are really so assured, so modern or even so scholarly.

Rather than a lone bleat crying in the wasteland of our age, this may be a voice from the heart of the flock. This member of the flock is not arrogant or idiotic enough to imagine that he is alone — many sheep are wandering as he did, searching for firm ground and a safe fold. He suspects that there are at least seven thousand who have not bowed the knee to the new idols shaped by theological scepticism. So perhaps the hopes, longings and the simple faith that dare not speak its name will find comfort in the words of this confession. Mere sheep should never be ashamed of their simplicity.

While sheep may not claim to be wise old owls, they can still dream, and who knows what dreams may come when they are huddled together against the chill winds of a cruel age and the blasts from a cold, academic theology? So between the chapters of this confession are a selection of such dreams, but in truth they can only be called nightmares. The twentieth century is an age of shattered dreams and, even in theology, has become an age of nightmares.

Finally, may this bleat turn to a plea? This simple sheep is not attacking any specific denomination or any particular minister who may have been called to be his shepherd. He respects them and, if it is any comfort to them, he freely confesses that he has often thanked God not to have been called to be a shepherd.

Nightmare
A liberal Luther

Your Imperial Majesty and your lordships demand
a simple answer. Here it is, plain and unvarnished.
I must be convinced by pure philosophy or the
pure reason of logical positivism — for I do not
accept the authority of the fundamentalist concept
of Scripture — the writers often contradict one
another.
My conscience is captive to the Word which lies
behind the Word — subject, of course, to the higher
and form criticism and a valid rational exegesis
which can become subjectively real to my existential experience.
So I will not and, with my academic presuppositions, cannot recant.
Here, subject to further research, I stand.
Ground of my being, help me.
Amen.

1
The Bible—I believe in the Bible

Perhaps I should tell it not in public and publish it not among the ranks of the theologians, but I believe the Bible — believe it with a simple faith which takes its words to be true, its history to be factual and all its claims to be authoritative. Rather than being a reasonable and respectable position for a Christian, this assertion is now greeted with an embarrassed silence; it is treated as a confession of ignorance, not of faith.

To say that the Bible is inspired, inerrant and infallible is to be met with raised eyebrows and pity for such simplicity. Such a view of Scripture is too simplistic for modern minds. Perhaps the primitive Jews could accept it as inspired and true, and such undeveloped minds as Jesus, Paul, Augustine, Athanasius, Tyndale, Wycliffe, Hus, Aquinas, Luther, Calvin, Knox, Newton, Pascal, Wesley, Shaftesbury, Wilberforce, Spurgeon and millions of others down through the centuries, but modern man is too intelligent for such simplicity.

So I am expected to rejoice in the fact that I am a son of the twentieth century, a child of the higher criticism, an off-spring of humanistic philosophy and the inheritor of modern science. Rather than open my Bible to read the very words of God, I am expected to approach it with critical faculties at the ready and to study the pages through the spectacles of scientific scepticism. This, I have been assured, is the only way to approach the Bible; whatever else I may do, I must not simply believe it. The Bible must be questioned, queried, doubted, investigated, analysed, dissected, parsed and generally treated like a corpse on a post-mortem table.

Of course, I am aware that this is all done in the name of

scholarly research to find the gold that lies hidden beneath the ravings of the prophets and the ramblings of Paul. The probe of modern intellectualism, the scalpel of imaginative insight and massive injections of humanistic criticism must be employed to understand the Bible in our age. Justification by faith has been replaced by justification by doubt; all things are up for question. The claim of the Bible to be the written revelation of God is implicitly, if not explicitly, denied and its own testimony of authority is set aside as being unworthy of serious thought. From Genesis to Revelation everything is up for debate and simple faith is treated with disdain.

Perhaps I may be forgiven for being both confused and bewildered at the lengthy things I must not believe if I want to be a Christian in the twentieth century. As I read and ponder the works of the modern liberal scholars I can only stand in puzzled amazement at how much of the 'old book' has gone and how little is left. Surely I cannot be the only one who, on seeing the bath water being thrown out, finds himself wondering what has happened to the baby?

Has God said?

I turn to the extreme liberals and find that they not only have got rid of the bath water and the baby, but have also discarded the bath. They have not so much reinterpreted the Bible my fathers knew, as demolished it until scarcely a memory remains.

The Mosaic authorship of the Pentateuch is disdainfully discarded and the whole chronological order of the Old Testament completely reorganized. They assure me that the Pentateuch was actually written by a number of people whom they know affectionately as J, E, D and P, and then someone with an early interest in jigsaws fitted the scraps together to make the first five books of the Bible.

Then, throughout the Old Testament, Darwin's biological theory is applied to the Jewish faith, so that instead of revelation, we have evolution. It is supposed to show a movement from primitive animism to Yahweh's becoming a tribal god until, under the prophets, monotheism eventually evolved. I must confess a suspicion that this was an application of the theory of evolution undreamt of by Charles Darwin, even in his wildest and most imaginative moments.

The New Testament is treated with equal ruthlessness and the Gospels are subjected to what can only be described as 'grievous bodily harm'. Matthew, Mark, Luke and John — if they existed — did not write their Gospels, and if they did then they got all the facts and events hopelessly wrong! They present Jesus as the incarnate God, a man who equated Himself with God, who forgave sins, did miracles, accepted the Old Testament as authoritative and true, died and physically rose again and will come again to judge the world. Of course, none of these things is in accordance with the findings of modern theology, so contemporary logic demands that it must be the Gospel records that are wrong — not the findings of modern man.

But it is not only the character and teaching of Jesus that is being challenged and denied: every doctrine is similarly treated. Doubt must be cast upon almost everything of importance in the Gospels. As the virgin birth does not agree with modern medical knowledge, it must be discarded. Miracles do not agree with contemporary scientific theories, so cannot be true. The substitutional death of Christ and His physical resurrection are not compatible with modern theories of justice or the 'facts' of science, so they must be denied. The ascension is obviously in direct contradiction to our understanding of astro-physics and cannot be accepted and, almost needless to add, Christ's coming again to judge and rule does not agree with process theology or evolutionary philosophy and must therefore be treated with academic disdain.

More than the Gospels have gone: the Epistles, too, must be treated as suspect. The letters of Peter, I am assured, are clever forgeries and, whoever wrote the Johannine Epistles, it was not John the apostle but some plastic replica of the same name. The Pauline writings were not written by Paul and scientific evidence has been produced to prove this — they have been submitted to the indignities of a computer. This has shown that they were not all written by the hand of Paul so, as a child of technology, I am expected to believe that the Word of God may err but the word of a computer is inerrant and infallible.

Of course all this means that the Bible is only occasionally right. The patriarchs were primitives; the prophets were unlearned; the Gospel writers naive and Paul usually got it all wrong. It is only when the writers of Scripture say something that is in complete agreement with contemporary theories that it can be considered as showing some resemblance to the truth.

These are the theories of the radical theologians, the avantgarde of the new thinkers; yet I must confess an uncomfortable suspicion that they are neither as new nor as modern as they would like to think. Indeed I have read about them in my Bible, in the early chapters of Genesis. In the Garden of Eden the first doubt was cast upon the Word of God, the first analytical criticism formulated and the first findings of the higher criticism were pronounced. There the serpent denied what God had said, analysing the supposed statement with rational logic to show that God did not mean what He said and that, if He did, then it must be wrong, because by disobeying they would not die but would become the equals of God by empirically knowing right and wrong.

The end result of being seduced by such clever theories was not an academic paradise but a world of sin, pain and death. Can I be condemned for fearing to tread such a path? When God speaks I want to listen; when He has spoken, I feel I must obey. Then, in my simplicity, I find it hard to believe that I should doubt the Word of God because the words of men contradict it — it seems to me more than possible that it is men who are wrong.

I find it simpler to believe the Bible and I am not alone in this belief; Jesus believed His Bible, the Old Testament, and I for one would hesitate to assert that I know more than He did. When tempted of Satan in the wilderness, Jesus replied three times, 'It is written. . . it is written. . . it is written. . . '

and the tempter was defeated. It seems a tragic commentary on our grim age that we now have those who would have answers to such simple statements.

'What is written,' they would say, 'and who wrote it, and why did he write it? What Babylonian and pagan myths influenced what he wrote? How can we prove we have what he wrote, and what has been added by redactors? And what existential interpretation should we put on it for today?' Perhaps if Satan had used such words it would have been my Lord who would have been silenced.

It is written. I believe it.

The Word: not the words

Other Christians, not so radical as the extreme liberals but apparently unable to share the simplicity of my faith, are also anxious to preserve the Bible as the Word of God. So they have told me about the Word which is behind the Word, and that truth lies in the Word and not in the words. They assure me that the Bible is just like an ordinary book with ordinary words, but in reading it, if I find it becoming real, confronting me with the challenge for commitment, then it is the Word which is behind the words that is communicating to me.

This may be clever and intellectual, but I must confess that it seems mystical and irrational to me. Perhaps it is my untutored mind, but I find the concept confusing, and tortuous questions swirl around my unbowed head. I find myself wondering if this is a new form of Platonic philosophy where the spiritual reality behind the material is the only true reality. Are the words of the Bible to be seen as Plato's forms — pale imitations of the true reality which is spiritual and beyond the material? Or are the words simply Kantian appearances behind which are the 'things in themselves'?

But it is not purely in the realms of philosophy that the questions arise in my mind; simple little questions dance before my eyes. Are the words necessary to communicate this Word? Or do the words of the Bible not really matter?

Then how can I know the truth of what this Word is saying to me? I may be simply imagining the whole thing! Can I measure the Word against the Word? But would not that mean that the words themselves must be true, otherwise how do I know the Word is true? Then, can it be said that there is a Word behind all words?

Already it can be clearly seen how my confusion is becoming confounded and I find myself being drawn into an infinite spiral where words become autonomous or function to control my view of reality. I am in danger of playing the Wittgensteinian language game where words are the beginning and end of philosophy and we never move beyond words.

So in my simplicity I take words to have meaning and my responsibility to lie in reading, marking and understanding. Then I am called to act on those words — to be a doer of the Word. I find nothing strange in the concept that God who made us verbal creatures, communicating through words, should communicate with us in words. So my position is plain and unashamed: I believe the Bible; I believe the words of the Bible. My heart seeks the truth, not in a mystical Word which can only be subjectively real, but in language which my poor and finite mind can understand. It is with thankfulness that I can not only rejoice in David's prayer, 'Thy Word is true' (Ps. 119:160), but can re-echo with triumph his assertion: 'Thy words are true' (2 Sam. 7:28).

No doubt many will see this as something approaching idolatry or, to use the modern jargon, an ideology. So I have been accused of worshipping a book rather than God and believing in propositions rather than a divine Person. In attempts to correct this fundamentalist malady or spiritual aberration, I have been advised to put my faith in God, and not in the Bible, and to trust Christ, not the pages of a book. No doubt such advice has been well meant even though I have seen no necessity for taking it.

If there is a clear distinction between believing God and believing His Word, then I must confess I have failed to see it. Perhaps it is very simplistic, but I cannot understand how I can trust someone and yet refuse to trust his word. If, as I

believe, the Bible is God's Word, then how can I say my faith
is in God, but have no faith in what He says? That would
really be to open the floodgates to idolatry.

Lest I be misunderstood, let me confess that my salvation
depends upon the grace of God and the finished work of
Christ on Calvary to procure redemption for lost sinners such
as I. But how do I know of the grace of God and the work of
Christ? I can read it in the pages of my Bible. Certainly I can
know something of the existential reality in my heart, but
how do I know my experience is valid and true — that I am
not just being led astray by my feelings, intuitions and
imagination? I can turn to Scripture and measure all things
against the words of truth.

History that is not history

There are those who would defend the authority of the Bible
against modern criticisms by retreating from a defence of its
essential historicity. Problems of creation, miracles and God's
open and spectacular intervention in human situations are
easily solved by making biblical history different from factual
history.

So I have been assured that my simple belief in the Bible
must be wrong because it does not contain history as men
know history. It records a form of supra-history; it is, to give
it its proper name, *Geschichte* — something that only becomes
real when it touches me existentially and demands commitment. Again this seems to be a clever way of making the
Bible immune from attacks from those who would question
the account of creation, the flood, passover, the wilderness
wanderings and even the events in the life of Jesus. There is
no need to debate; they can be silenced by the assertion that
all this is not history — it is *Geschichte*. So the Christian faith
and the Bible can be kept as historical by making them into a
different kind of history.

Perhaps it shows the sluggishness of my mind, but I must
confess a complete inability to operate such a skilled
Orwellian 'double-think'. Like every schoolboy, I take

history to be facts and events that happened to real people at a particular time; anything else I would take to be fiction. Not only that, but I have a childish curiosity to know what happened, and rather suspect that most men share this desire for factual knowledge. Then I have the simple belief that things either happened or did not happen and, if this should sound too childish a proposition, I could restate it as a basic tenet of logic that A cannot be non-A.

This is why the very idea that biblical history is not true history is mentally disorientating to me. Either Adam and Eve were real persons, or they were not; either Abraham and Moses lived, or they did not; either the prophets lived and preached, or they did not; and either Jesus was born of a virgin, did miracles, rose from the dead, or He did none of these things. I cannot take them to be both true and not true. If these things, and all the events recorded in Scripture, were not true in real history, but only in some transcendent form of mystical history, then I suspect that to believe them is to believe a lie.

An even more disturbing problem for me in this concept, that biblical history is different history, is the fact that the writers seem to have been under the impression that they were recording factual events in real situations. So the prophets date their ministries by naming kings and quoting natural events, such as earthquakes and famines, to reveal the historical setting of their ministry.

I can only pity poor Luke, who did not seem to be aware that he was writing a completely different type of history when he explained his system of historical research in the prologue to his Gospel. He dates the birth of Jesus Christ by giving the names of the Caesar and the Governor of Syria, and the event of a political census; he goes into even greater details when he dates the beginning of John's ministry, giving the year of Tiberius Caesar's reign, and lists the names of the Governor of Judea, the Kings of Galilee, Ituraea, Abilene, and the high priest. I must confess that in reading the words of Luke, like those of all the biblical writers, I have the impression that they were recording factual events which took place in real time among real people.

In spite of all efforts to educate me to the contrary, I find it easier, and more logically intellectual, just to believe the Bible as it is written. I can find no comfort or academic sanity in seeing the Scripture twisted and rewritten to suit the latest theories and ideas of mere men, reducing them to an interesting collection of old documents. Indeed, if the modern theologians are right, then it seems to me more than doubtful that the Bible should be considered a 'good' book — how can it be good when it has deceived so many people for so long? I am expected to believe that God, the Fountain of all truth and light, allowed His people to be misled and deceived for centuries, allowing them to see lies as truth, miracles as facts, history as reality, and letting them think that all that it records and affirms is utterly trustworthy and true.

Perhaps I will be dismissed as a nostalgic romantic who is afraid to face the reality of the twentieth century. Yet I would contend that I am holding, not only to the historical orthodox faith, but to the only truly rational position for any intelligent man of my generation; it is neither incredible nor incomprehensible. If men can make electric lights, I cannot see anything irrational in believing in a God who made the sun; if men can communicate verbally, I can see no reason for refusing to believe in a God who communicates through words. My Bible-believing position is that of the open mind — open to God and the reality of His creation; it is those who deny or modify the Word of God who suffer from the affliction of the closed mind. Miracles are a good illustration of this point.

Those of liberal theological persuasion must find it an embarrassment that the Bible is a book of miracles. Seas part and leave dry land; a rod is turned into a snake; the dead are raised; an axehead floats on water, and Jesus can make even the wind and the waves obey Him. Now it is an obvious fact that miracles do not fit easily into the secularized mind of the twentieth century, but it is ironic that modern man will confidently assert that this is the age of miracles — he accepts the miracles of men but denies the miracles of God. I have more than a suspicion that this sort of thinking is the result of a closed mind.

My criticism of such doubt is that it does not go far enough and apparently accepts as infallible and inerrant the arguments of the patron saint of sceptics, David Hume, who contended that it was more likely that reports of miracles were wrong than that they actually happened and, anyway, the laws of nature denied the possibility of the miraculous. Everything must be doubted — except the laws of nature!

Again questions swarm around my mind. How do we know that miracles never happen? What authority have we for such an assertion? If they are scientifically impossible, what conceivable experiment can we set up to prove the theory? Is our understanding of the laws of nature so complete and comprehensive that it can be proved to be a completely 'closed system'? In an age of quantum physics and relativity, would any reputable scientist dare to assert that there is no possible way in which the common course of events could be set aside and a miracle occur?

The truth is that those who start with the assumption that miracles do not take place have closed their minds to certain things. They have closed their minds to the possibility of God's acting in a special and unique way in history; they either assert that God *cannot* do miracles — an astonishing assumption, or that He *will* not do miracles — an equally astonishing assumption in that it claims to know the will and purpose of God. Of course a common way out is to seek to embrace the best of both worlds: to accept miracles which can be explained in terms of modern scientific knowledge and reject the rest — in other words, if I cannot understand it, then it did not happen. I hardly think that can be claimed to be a very good example of the open mind.

These arguments on miracles apply to the whole of the Bible. It seems to me to be a clear example of the closed mind to read the words of Scripture and only accept what is agreeable to contemporary theology or philosophy. I reject as unworthy and unacademic putting the pages of the Bible in a hat and only picking out those which are in accordance with the modern mind. If parts of the Bible are legend, how do I know that it is not all legend? If creation is a saga, how can I be sure that my redemption by Christ on the cross is not equally a saga? If I cannot trust some of the pages, then how can I trust the rest?

So it seems to me to be much simpler and safer to believe the Bible as it is written rather than the words of modern man. I find it disturbing and confusing to hear the siren voices of the contemporary theologians who, beginning with reason, rationalism, existentialism, Marxism, dialectic materialism, or just old-fashioned imagination, seek to rewrite the Word of God. In seeking to make that Word contemporary and acceptable for our age they have complicated it beyond all measure and understanding.

The failure of the new Bible

It seems to me that the whole enterprise has failed. All attempts to demythologize the Bible or reinterpret it liberally have been made with what are claimed to be the highest motives — to make it more acceptable to, and easily understood by modern man. So, now that we have had over a century of higher criticism and the various rational, mythological and existential reinterpretations, what has been the result?

Are more people clamouring to read this new Bible? Are our churches crowded? Are the members more learned, more theologically aware, more saintly and more Christian than any previous generation? Perhaps I will not be considered arrogant if I express my doubts. I suspect that the evidence points in the opposite direction. It has simply confused the faithful, making them almost ashamed of their simple faith, and has not reached out into the world of those who know little of God and the gospel of grace.

It seems to me that, rather than welcoming and accepting this new Bible the average man rejects it as being basically dishonest. Not being trained in the art of double-think he finds it exceedingly difficult to accept lies as being truth, historical accounts as being really myths and assertions of miraculous happenings as being simple parables. In his simple rationality, if he reads the Bible, he assumes it simply means what it says; he may refuse to believe, but works on the valid assumption that it is there to be accepted or denied, not that it is really an intellectually religious crossword full of cryptic clues which can only be solved by those armed with the latest theological thesaurus. So if he reads that Jesus rose from the dead, that the disciples saw Him, touched Him, had a meal with Him, then he rightly assumes that it is claiming that a man rose from the dead. Of course, he may deny this as a historical fact, but he will not understand it as really a philosophical truth enshrined in a myth which has nothing to do with a deceased body being restored to life.

Indeed, I suspect that the very words beloved by the modern theologian — 'myth . . . legend . . . saga . . . parable . . .' are equated with fairy stories and idle tales in the minds of most contemporary people. They probably believe it is simply academic language for saying that the Bible is 'bunk'. The suspicion has grown that science, which is capable of exploding the atom, has exploded the Bible, and the further work of demolition is now being taken over by the teachers of theology. I cannot be the only one who wonders whether this has anything to do with our rapidly degenerating culture. If the Bible is not to be trusted, then God seems to move further and further away, and not only are all things up for question, but all answers become merely a matter of opinion.

After all, why should men pay attention to the Ten Commandments, when they are told that the laws of Hammurabi are just as good as the law of Moses? Why should men follow the ethical teaching of Jesus if no one is sure what He said or did, and the Gospels are seen as the collective theological imagination of the early church? Why should anyone turn to the Bible to learn of freedom and liberty, if the teachings of Marx are equally valid as a liberating theology? If there is no Word of truth, do we not end with all men doing that which is right in their own eyes?

It seems to me that the very attempt to demythologize and existentialize the Bible, rather than being modern, is failing because it is old-fashioned. It is the reaction of those who have not only lost their nerve in the face of the advance of modern secularism, but also are completely out of touch with contemporary man and the real agonies of people trapped in our one-dimensional world. It is based on the quaint idea that twentieth-century man, living in the closed universe of a materialistic culture, does not want to know anything of a transcendent reality or a spiritual plane. So the basic premiss of the liberal approach is to make Christianity acceptable by bringing it down to the level of the material and practical, to make it philosophically verifiable and scientifically respectable.

Does not such a view manifest a total lack of understanding of what is happening in the materialistic world of our post-Christian culture? Far from modern man being at home in a one-dimensional world, his real problem is to find a way to escape from it. So he is struggling and striving to find some means of transcending materialistic nihilism, which has become destructive of life and a prison-house for the soul. So the idols of our age multiply — sex, drugs, pop, politics, new Eastern religions, mysticism, sport and all the many other things men seek to use to escape the plastic-coated culture which they have created.

The eternal God of the Scriptures, Creator, Sovereign and Saviour, when brought down to the level of the twentieth century is no God, and the Bible, reduced to the supposed requirements of modern man, ends by being no Bible because it has no good news. Man cannot live by academic bread alone, or find life in the cakes of the welfare state — there must be something 'other', something 'beyond' to give meaning and purpose to life. It seems obvious to me that the coldly rational, materialistic, scientifically verifiable Bible of the modern liberal theologians cannot answer the questions and longings that are throbbing in the heart of modern man.

Man does not need a new way and a new truth to give him life — the answer spoken so long ago in the upper room is still valid today. So, rather than being encouraged to wander as he will, believing what he likes, he needs to be shown the way. A desert without map or compass must be a terrifying experience, and the waste land of the twentieth century is littered with pilgrims who are being led by false prophets.

Although it may be simplistic, I will hold to the view that there is a guidebook for all of us travelling the roads of life. The Bible, God's Word written, is that book which gives light and directions, and if that is not to be trusted then all is lost. After all, if God has spoken, is His Word not true? Is it no longer valid for our age? It seems to me that to ask those questions is to know the answer.

The Bible is an anvil which has worn out many a hammer. I have no fear that it will not outlive all its current critics, because I have on the highest authority the assurance that, although heaven and earth may pass away, the Word of God will stand for ever. I see no need to alter, change, water down and seek to make more palatable for modern taste the Bible, which is still sharper than any two-edged sword and alone is profitable for teaching the truth, rebuking errors, correcting faults and giving instruction in right living.

Perhaps it is the romantic in me, but I do confess that I find it inspiring to look back and learn from the lives of those who simply believed the Bible. Can any deny that in days gone by there were many mighty men who, daring to believe the Bible, were giants in faith and action? In a fallen world, where all things are tainted by sin, sometimes they may have been narrow-minded and bigoted and occasionally wrong, yet their works live after them. They fought for liberty and justice for all; they campaigned to free slaves and give children the right of childhood; they rescued fallen women and lost men; they founded hospitals, schools, orphanages and old people's homes; they established missionary societies and charities and were active in all the arts and sciences. They lived and died trusting in the words of God.

In fairness, I should confess, the new generation, educated by all the contortions and confusions of modern liberal theology, may well also be ready to live and die for their faith. They may well be willing to go to the stake for the truth of the Wellhausen hypothesis or the truth of Q and form criticism, living and dying for the Word behind the Word or the existential reality of historical myths, but I find myself wondering. I have the uncomfortable feeling that I live in an age of small men with tiny visions and little faith and, if indeed they are great, then it can only be said that they are great and mighty in doubt.

It may well be that I will be considered a fool in the land of the wise and a simpleton amid the learned, but I make no apology, believing that it is the fear of the Lord that is the beginning of wisdom. It is only by beginning with God and His Word that we can be truly wise and have understanding. So in my simplicity I accept that God has spoken and, rather than sit in judgement on that Word, I submit myself with the humble prayer of the prophet: 'Speak, Lord, thy servant heareth.'

Nightmare
A new Paul

Ye men who have come of age, I perceive that in all things ye are too religious. For as I passed by and beheld your devotions I saw many churches with this inscription: 'To the glory of God'.
Whom therefore ye ignorantly worship, him declare I unto you.
For we now know that God did not make the world and all things therein, seeing that such a belief would contradict the truth of the cosmic Big Bang and the dogma of evolution. Neither is he worshipped with men's hands as if he had anything to do with us.
And all the nations of the world have been made by natural selection and their times appointed and the bounds of their habitation fixed by economic determinism and the forces of social and cultural progress. For it is in this we live and move and have our being.
Now, as certain of your own poets have said, 'It is as atheistic to affirm the existence of God as it is to deny it.' And again, 'He is to be found in the depths of our being.'
Seeing therefore we are the offspring of this unknown God we ought not to think of him as sovereign, almighty or a loving heavenly Father, but seek him beyond both being and non-being.
For God has appointed a day in which men will

come of age by that man for others whom he has
ordained, whereof he has given assurance unto all
men in that he has given us the legends of the
Gospels and the myth of a man dying and rising
again.

2
God—I believe in God

'I believe in God,' begins the Apostles' Creed and, without the mental reservations and linguistic qualifications beloved by much modern theology, I assent willingly to the confession. Such a belief is eminently respectable and certainly academically necessary; after all, we are told that it is only a fool who would say there is no God. Then there is nothing specifically Christian about believing in the existence of God: there is scriptural authority for asserting that even the devils believe.

Not only do I believe in God, but I dare to claim that I know Him — the living God. I know Him through the simplicity of faith and, through grace, have been brought into a new and living relationship with Him. Of course, ever conscious of my own finiteness and the limitations of my own understanding, I am fully aware that my knowledge cannot be exhaustive or comprehensive — how can the finite fully comprehend the infinite? It is simplicity, not arrogance, that makes me believe I can know God; I have found Him, not through the higher reaches of speculative philosophy or the distortions of liberal theology, but through the fact that He has revealed Himself to the simple in heart, the humble and the meek. The heavens declare His glory and the wonders of earth show forth His handiwork; all of creation is a revelation of the God who made all things. Then He has spoken in the enscriptured Word, revealing the depths of His grace and the breadth of His love and, finally, in Christ Jesus, His Son, He has shown us Himself.

Perhaps this is too simple for the intelligent beings of the

twentieth century, but it is enough for me. Through His grace
and by His Spirit, I can know God. Yet I must confess, perhaps thereby revealing the extent of my ignorance, that when
I turn to books of learned theology written by those of the
modern liberal school, I have the terrifying sensation that one
requires an honours degree in philosophy, some degrees in
theology and a doctorate in linguistics to know God. The
God of my fathers, Creator and Sovereign, Saviour and
Friend, loving and fatherly, seems to have gone from the
minds and hearts of those who would teach me the faith and
lead the way.

The unknown God

To talk of God in the modern theological climate is to find
oneself caught in a maze of mind-blowing speculation and to
be carried away in a whirlwind of irrationalism; concepts and
phantasies abound, each more daring and incomprehensible
than the other and, to state the obvious, all is confusion.
Whatever the simple-hearted such as myself may think,
biblical terminology is no longer adequate either to know or
to address God. So in the jargon of contemporary thought it
is not enough to think of God as the Creator, the God and
Father of the Lord Jesus Christ, or the sovereign God of love
and grace. He is to be understood as the Wholly Other, the
Ground of our being, the Ultimate Concern, the Transcendental Reality, the Existing Factor, the First Cause, the
Universal Constant, or 'Something'. Whatever else I must do,
I cannot simply call Him 'Father'.

Indeed we seem to have come to the point where we cannot speak of God at all. The psalmist may have thought it
foolish to say there is no God, but what am I to make of a
Christian theologian who has assured me in his works that it
is as foolish to say there is a God as to say there is no God? I
must see that He is 'beyond being'. I can only take this to
mean that God is really an abstraction, a concept and not a
reality, and the words of the psalm should be reinterpreted to
read: 'The fool has said in his heart, there is no God; and the

other fool answers, there is a God.'

It is here that I must be wrong. I am taking the creational and written revelation as revealing a God who is infinite and personal; modern theology, with its new insights, is seeking to show me that the old categories and classifications are no longer valid. God has become a philosophical principle, not a person, an academic abstraction, not the living God. The very word 'God' has become meaningless. Indeed, I have come across the delightfully ironic suggestion that we should stop using the word for at least a generation!

Such a proposition appeals to my sense of the ridiculous and my imagination conjures up the most idiotic consequences that would arise if such a suggestion was adopted. Religious bookshops would be emptied of their contents, Christian journals would have to be devoted to the secular saints or the theology of Marx and Engels, and modern playwrights would find it a handicap in limiting their casual blasphemies. But what about the church? A service of public worship where God is never mentioned would be a most interesting, if not bewildering, experience.

The call to worship would begin with a fresh transcription of the old words and would have to be something like, 'Let us worship the name we dare not speak.' I have not done any research on the subject but should imagine that it would be exceedingly difficult to find psalms and hymns where God is not mentioned, so congregational singing would have to be severely restricted. Prayers would present a real problem but perhaps the gathered congregation could be encouraged to bow their heads and meditate on the grounds of their being — though I have the suspicion that the average member would find the experience confusing, if not simply idiotic.

Bible readings would have to be carefully selected, probably the easiest course would be to concentrate on the books of Esther and Song of Solomon where the name of God is not used; there would be the added advantage that, after a time, the congregation would be fully conversant with these two unfamiliar parts of Scripture. Probably the easiest part of such a service would be the sermon where a cosy little

homily could be presented. Undemanding, little, morally up-
lifting talks are always permissible and certainly safer; it was
when the prophets ignored popular little homilies and started
proclaiming the Word of God that they found themselves
being stoned.

Of course the simplest way out of the difficulty of avoiding the name of God would be to abolish church services
altogether. Everyone could stay at home, sitting with due
reverence before the television set, singing the latest pop
songs or advertising jingles, and paying homage to electronics
and the wonders man has done.

Perhaps that is enough of my satirical wanderings, but my
sanity is still threatened by the views and theories of those
who would teach me how to be a real Christian in the
modern secularized world. They have the ability to be con-
tinually amazing me with their latest theories which seem to
cover the whole spectrum of human thought from the god
who is not God to his sudden death a few years ago and now
his apparent resurrection as a disciple of Karl Marx.

Pascal was of the opinion that the god of the philosophers
was not the God of the Bible. It is not too much to assert
that if he was living today he would amend his statement to
read that the god of the modern theologians is not the God
of the Bible. The problem for simple souls such as myself is
to see and understand the real difference between the views
of some liberal theologians and the humanistic philosophers.
Once upon a time theology was considered to be the queen
of the sciences but now, I rather suspect, it is little more than
a pet poodle faithfully — or faithlessly — following the steps
of the intellectual trend-setters. Rather than confronting the
errors of the age, it embraces them; rather than debating the
theories of men, it accepts them, and rather than leading, it
seems to follow blindly wherever the latest ideas may lead. It
can be no surprise that in this situation, and considering the
reaction, God seems afar off and completely unknown.

Perhaps there are great blessings to be had if one is simple
and believes with Paul that it is in God that we live and move
and have our being. We can know Him, love Him, serve Him

— which is more than I can do for the god of modern theology who seems to be a vague, nebulous force, an indefinible Other beyond the reaches of my heart.

The disappearing God

Even within the severe limitations of my intellectual capacity, I am fully aware that the growing secularization of all of life cannot be wholly laid upon the unbowed head of the liberal theologians of my century. The process started a long time ago (in truth it can be traced back to the Garden of Eden when man first wanted to live without God) but the modern movement really began in the period which, ironically, is known as the Enlightenment. It was then the seeds of the modern secular society were first sown and human reason, rather than revelation or theology, became both king and queen of all the sciences.

Then, as men's knowledge of the universe increased, they were able to devise bigger and better theories about all things. Slowly the concept of the biblical God was discarded as an unnecessary hindrance to the thinking and dreams of men. Knowledge became more scientific, more positivistic, and the very idea of a God who had to reveal Himself became almost an affront to 'reason'. So the very idea of the God who made heaven and earth, upholding the creation every moment of time, Sovereign and Saviour, Author of the Bible and Miracle-Worker, was dismissed as unreasonable. Although the philosophers may have used the word 'God', it was no longer the God of the Bible or the orthodox Christian faith, but the god of the philosophers, the unknown god of the deists, or the 'Supreme Reason' of some of the French revolutionaries. Laplace wanted a hypothesis which had no need of God and, over the years since the Enlightenment, humanists have sought to produce that thesis. Today the vision of that dream still haunts men and among them, I suspect, there are those who would claim to be Christian scholars.

Now a strange trinity of prophets occupies the dark heavens of the modern world, and the stars of Darwin, Marx and Freud dazzle the eyes and hide from view the God our fathers knew. They have brought a new revelation which seems to dominate the world-view and thought patterns of modern man. The dream of Laplace seems to have come to pass: God has been banished from the universe.

Darwin succeeded in dismissing the concept of God the Creator and Sustainer of all things. All of life became a matter of natural selection and creatures evolving to suit their environment. Life was not created by the Word of God but by the chance meeting of energy and matter — even though modern physics cannot distinguish between matter and energy, the basic thesis still holds good: God is not needed. He is not be be found in the Big Bang or the Steady State theory. Evolution became the answer and the key to the understanding of life — of all creation. God, the Creator, became irrelevant.

Karl Marx succeeded in abolishing the God of history. The concept of the God who reigns on high, governing all things according to His will, was denied. Everything in human life became a matter of dialectic materialism, merely a matter of economics, class struggles and the blind forces of history working for the proletariat. God had nothing to do with the workings of His world; indeed His very revelation was merely an opiate for the masses.

Freud then sought to abolish the concept of the Father God who cares for His children. Man was no longer to be seen as a creature created in the image of God, but was a frightened, immature being comprising id, ego and super-ego who had created a god in his own image. Man was afraid of the hostile universe, living in terror of the dark and the strong forces within him, so he created in his own imagination a cosmic father to whom he could turn for help or whom he could blame for the ills of life. To believe in God became an admission of failure, a confession of immaturity. God was not a reality, but a sick dream.

To avoid any accusations of intellectual dishonesty, I must admit that I am not as naive or simplistic as to imagine that these are the precise or complete teachings of Darwin, Marx and Freud. I am aware that they all had valuable things to say, but I would assert that the things I have outlined have been the effect of their teachings on the common mind of my generation. More than that, I suspect that they are also the presuppositions which lie behind much of what passes for modern theology.

With God pushed out of the creation and the great movements and life of men, much more than God vanished. Everything was called into question and the universe became a lonely place. I can find it in my heart to pity with a great pity poor Nietzsche who could cry in the market-place of the world, 'God is dead, and we have killed him!' Of course he ended up in a mental asylum. Yet less than a century later 'Christian' theologians were taking up the same cry as Nietzsche and, rather than being committed as insane, they were fêted and probably grew rich from producing weighty tomes in which they wrote the obituaries of the almighty and living God. Let me confess I find it hard to pity such men who, as servants of God, expressed their faith by announcing His sudden demise. Emotions are always complex and sometimes contradictory, so my reaction to the 'death of God' school of modern theology consisted of being amazed, angry, puzzled, amused, horror-stricken, bewildered, surprised and perplexed.

Yet, while it is obviously absurd to think of God — the Giver of all life — as being dead, the truth of the matter is that God does seem to have departed from our age. All things seem to function without God and all the arts and sciences will, at the drop of a hat, willingly produce a hypothesis which has no need of God and no room for God. We now seem to inhabit a world created by Darwin, governed by Marx and sustained by Freud.

So the God of the Bible, my God, is farther than ever away from the mind and thinking of the secular world of the twentieth century. It is accepted that the world came into being without God, that all things work without God and that all things can be explained without God. Modern man is educated and brought up to be proud and arrogant, puffed up with his own achievements and encouraged to look back with pity and laughter on the primitive generations who believed, prayed and trusted their Bible and the God of the Bible. No longer do the heavens declare the glory of God, they show the sputniks and spacecraft of almighty man. Man no longer needs God; he can now take over his own evolution and conquer the universe.

Rather than confronting these idiotic and sinful romantic assumptions, it seems to me that many Christian thinkers are almost in complete agreement with them; indeed they have added to the illusion of grandeur by telling us that man has come of age and can do without the God in whom our fathers trusted. Instead of holding to the God of the revealed Word they have sought to redefine the Almighty and, as was to be expected, have only succeeded in making Him into an intellectual and verbal abstraction. But, even more dangerous than that, they have made God into a moral irrelevancy.

Perhaps this is why the god of modern liberal theology has his attractions to many; he is not a God who makes demands and challenges our hearts. A god who is a 'God behind God' or is 'Wholly Other' or a 'First Cause' is nicely and comfortably vague and distant; at all times he must remain safely remote and happily obscure. He cannot be a God who demands justice and righteousness, who gives laws and commandments and will not look upon iniquity. He is not a God of judgement and grace.

Indeed I suspect he is not a god at all, but must remain the product of sinful speculation, a distant abstraction which is nothing more than the devising of men's hearts. Rather than God searching the heart of man we now have men daring to search God, reducing Him to the level of their own finite minds and seeking to confine Him into moulds of their own making.

The world may go on as if God did not exist, men may deny His existence and mock His claims but, as is well known, men can be wrong. There is a God, and although all the fools in the world got together and cried in unison, 'There is no sun, there is no sun,' the sun would continue to shine. Though all the intellectual fools of our age may deny and mock the concept of God, He still reigns, God over all. It is only men who refuse to lift up their eyes who would dare to say, 'There are no stars.'

The God I know

I believe that I know something of this great and terrible God who is rich in grace and mercy. I believe I know, not through the dazzling brilliance of my intellect, or through my being conversant with all the latest theories and concepts, but because He has revealed Himself. This revelation is there for all those who humble themselves and look with the eyes of faith, recognizing that the fear of the Lord is the beginning of wisdom. Can there be a more profound or greater wisdom than knowing God?

I would say that I have learned something of God in the works of His hands — not in the creation revealed to me in the works of Darwin, but in the creation of which I am part. I see, with a sense of wonder, the complexity and simplicity of all things: the sun, moon and stars; the trees, fruits and flowers; the birds and beasts and fish — all the works of His hands. Perhaps I shall be accused of being a latter-day disciple of Paley, but behind the design I see a Designer. I see the handiwork of God in the vein of a leaf, the shape and colour of a flower, the migration of birds, the unity of the ecosphere, the cycle of the planets and even in the wrinkled face of an old woman or the bright curious eyes of a child. I am surrounded by His glory and the manifold works of His hands. In all things I see the diversity and unity, beauty and strength, order and freedom which is in God's creation.

But it is not simply a romantic love of nature or an aesthetic appreciation of beauty that reveals the God of creation to my eyes and understanding. I can see His glory revealed in the very works of men's hands. All that men have and all that they are capable of doing are but gifts from His hands; they are part of the creational possibilities which our Creator God has bestowed. So in all the arts and sciences, in all the thoughts and imaginations of men, in all their organizations and affairs, I still see something of the power, wonder and glory of God. He is the Giver of all gifts and has given them to all men, both righteous and unrighteous, to show something of His goodness to the children of men.

So even atheistic militants, like the Russians, sending men into space and assuring me that God is not to be found there, can only make me laugh them to scorn. The intellectual, mathematical and technological capability which enabled them to leave the planet earth were all gifts from God. Without Him they could do nothing.

To me it is valid to say that I can know something of God through His creation; the heavens do declare the glory of God and the earth, in spite of the curse of sin, is still charged with His presence. But I am not limited to the creation to learn something of Him; He has communicated through His Word. Again, without apologies for my simplicity, I would confess that I take the Bible to be the verbalized Word of God.

It seems to me to be philosophically and psychologically absurd to suggest that we can get to know a person without talking and listening to him. In spite of the theories of the behaviourists, we are not non-verbal communicators sniffing around one another like animals; we were made to talk and listen. Therefore it is perfectly reasonable to assume that the God who made us verbal creatures should verbally communicate to us. 'Thus saith the Lord,' is one of the most frequent phrases in the Bible and I take it to mean exactly what it says: God is speaking and I must listen. Needless to add, I take it as self-evident that His Word and His words are true. Would an infallible God speak to us through fallible means?

So I learn of God through His Word. Rather than a humanistic theory of progressive evolution in the religious thought of the Jewish people, I take the Bible to be God's unfolding revelation, disclosing Himself to His people and, through them, to all mankind.

Here I can learn of a God who made all things, not simply the material and physical world, the Maker of all things visible and invisible. He is not a mechanic who wound up the clock of the universe and then busied himself with other affairs; He is not an explosive expert who set the fuse for the Big Bang and then waited to see the result, but a Creator who not only made, but upholds the creation day by day, moment by moment, a God in whom we live and move and have our being. He is the God who made all things seen and unseen — mountains and gravity, planets and dreams, oceans and atoms, wind and infinite space. The Bible tells me they are all the works of His hands.

Then it is from the Bible I learn that my intuitional feelings that things are not as they ought to be, or indeed as they were meant to be, are really true. It was not a sinful, struggling, suffering world which God made or is making. God made all things well and saw that it was very good. It was not a failed creation or an evil world which God made — it was perfect. Man was created to be in complete harmony and in perfect relationship with God, nature and himself. But, as the Bible tells me, sin entered and all the fair creation fell with man.

Although it may seem simplistic to many who would be wise, I must confess that a historical Fall seems a theological and philosophical necessity to make sense of the world in which I live and the whole of God's written revelation. The recurring themes in Scripture of redemption, reconciliation and restoration imply this Fall. How can you redeem that which has never been lost, reconcile those which have never been parted or restore that which has never existed before? So the Garden of Eden I see as no myth, legend or religious parable, but a historical place which saw a historical event and remains as the race memory of a golden age which haunts all men, torturing them with the thought of what might have been and what had been intended. Perhaps the historicity of Genesis may be considered unworthy of serious attention by those who are wise in their own conceits, but I must confess that to me the biblical record is more rational and logical than all the fine theories which men love to spin as they sit around the tribal fire or muse in their book-lined studies.

The same Bible, in its revelation of God, shows me that

even after the Fall, God still loved the world. It shows a God who is concerned with the affairs of men, who demands justice and righteousness, mercy and love: a God who hates sin and yet loves the sinner, who is not willing that any should perish, but desires all men to turn to Him and live. He so loves the world that He sent His only begotten Son so that whosoever may believe in Him should not perish but should have everlasting life.

So I can know something of God through His Word — the God of grace and judgement, who makes the sun to shine on the just and the unjust, and is kind to the rebellious as well as the religious. It tells me that His works are never a failure but that, through Christ, He will make all things anew; all that has been lost through sin will be restored and redeemed and there will be a new heaven and a new earth wherein will dwell righteousness.

If all this is unthinking fundamentalism or religious romanticism, then I plead guilty. If I am accused of being unable to decipher the rich mythologies of the Bible, which are supposed to show ultimate concern, transcendental reality or the one beyond being, then willingly, indeed happily, I confess the accusation. I am a simple soul who believes the Bible and finds there a knowledge of the God who made me, cares for me, sent His Son to die for my sins and has promised never to leave or forsake me.

It is in the same Bible I can learn of Jesus, of Him who was the Word of God made flesh. The God who has spoken by prophets and saints has spoken most clearly of all in His Son. There is a sense in which Jesus Christ is God's last word to men.

To see Jesus is to see God. I take this, not as a proposition of speculative philosophy or merely a theological concept, but as a simple fact which was claimed by Jesus Himself. 'He that has seen me has seen the Father,' were his own words. So through, and in, Christ I can come to know God as One who loves and cares for all men and came to earth to rescue the fallen. All are important to Him, the rich and the poor, the learned and the ignorant; the woman at the well and the righteous Nicodemus were treated with the same courtesy and compassion. I can see a God who heals, gives grace, faith, hope and love to all who come to Him in repentance and simple faith.

In all these areas — the creation of which I am part, the words of Scripture and, above all, in the person of His Son — I can know and learn something of God. Perhaps this God is not the God of the philosophers or the liberal theologians, but He seems to me to be the living God who lives and reigns for ever. If I listen to the other voices of our age, then I must find no God who can be real and relevant, or bring peace and grace to my troubled soul. Those who look at creation with evolutionary-coloured spectacles, read the Bible with a serpent-like insinuation, 'Has God said?' and reduce Jesus Christ to a figment of existential reality — how can they know God? Indeed, if they are right then we cannot know God. The word 'God' becomes meaningless and the ignorance is hidden in the smokescreen of technical jargon or in the mists of a contorted and confused phraseology.

'Let God be God,' pleads Paul and, in simplicity and intellectual humility, I can only re-echo the words. But, sadly, such advice is largely ignored today. In the proud building of new theological towers of Babel men are seeking to drag God down to meet the requirements of rationalistic philosophy, to make Him fit the new moulds of existential or revolutionary theology. I rather suspect that they are indulging in the old sin of seeking to banish God from the universe, or at least from the realm of human affairs. After all, there is no doubt that a holy God is an uncomfortable God, and to confess that we are rebellious sinners, whose very intellects are suspect and corrupt, is very humiliating. Perhaps it is not surprising that men do not want God to be God.

Some time ago a book was published with the arresting title of *The God I Want*. It was interesting but, to me at least, it was also disturbing in ways which were probably not intended by the contributors. While it may be intellectually stimulating and invigorating to discuss the kind of God we would like, what is really challenging and truly awesome is to turn to the Word of God and see the kind of man God wants — that is really the crucial question. In the final analysis we cannot pick and choose — God is God.

So I must end with the words with which I began this chapter, the assertion in the Apostles' Creed: 'I believe in God.' Surely I am not the only one who thinks he knows what he means when he repeats those words. I am not arrogant or foolish enough to claim that my knowledge is either exhaustive or complete; I can only see through a glass darkly. But I do know in whom I have believed. . .

Nightmare
A new Jesus

I believe in the historical Jesus Christ, who was not the Son of God, was not conceived by the Holy Ghost, nor born of the virgin Mary. Suffered under Pontius Pilate, was crucified, dead and buried. He did not descend into hell, the third day he did not rise from the dead, and he did not ascend into heaven.
Now he sitteth not on the right hand of God the Father, from whence he will not come to judge the quick and the dead.

3
Jesus—I believe in Jesus

I believe in Jesus and doubtless this is quite acceptable to all and sundry; it is only when I spell out what I mean by the confession that hackles arise and barriers are erected. Yet there can be no doubt that Jesus Christ is not simply a figure of history; He has torn the history of men asunder and has influenced and shaped cultures and nations for almost two thousand years. Long ago men crucified Him, and down through the generations many attempts have been made to banish His name from the lips of men, and yet He is still in the midst of all of life, challenging and judging.

The story of the life of Jesus has appealed to the greatest of scholars, because His life and teaching have a profundity and breadth which challenge the greatest minds and give scope for the deepest study. Yet they have an appeal to the simple and can delight the heart of a little child. I see no contradiction here; at the heart of things perhaps it is the simple things which are most profound and profundity has an essential simplicity.

Perhaps it will be taken as proof of my credulity if I confess how I see the story of Jesus. I believe in the Incarnation, the truth rather than the myth of God incarnate. So I accept that God was made flesh and dwelt among us, walking the dusty roads of earth, and His name was Jesus. He lived, did mighty works, died and rose again and is now in heaven until the day when He returns to take His own into the Father's kingdom. I am fully aware that it is a simple story and I first learned it at my mother's knee and from the stories read by my father. In growth to understanding and maturity I have been able to read it for myself, studying and meditating and finding it to be true to my own experience and knowledge of life. But I take it to be true, not because of my experience or emotions — they can lead astray — but because it is in the Bible. So, unashamedly, I love the gospel story and believe it to be true.

The Jesus of imaginative history

But what has happened to that story which my father loved and my mother cherished? It has all been superseded with the arrogance of a barren intellectualism which has destroyed, rather than made plain, and which has explained away, rather than revealed. The facts of the life of Jesus have vanished into the mists of poetry, myth, legends, dreams or the collective drama that was the product of the collective faith of the early church. Today the Gospel records are not considered sufficiently valid for modern man, so it was necessary to find the real Jesus — one who could be equated with the twentieth century. It was assumed that the Jesus of faith must be totally different from the Jesus of history.

So the Gospels have been analysed and scrutinized with all the tools that humanistic philosophy could apply. The results, considering the presuppositions which lay behind the enterprise, were not surprising but they certainly are radical.

The Incarnation account has been relegated to the level of a fairy story with Herod as the big bad king. Now apparently nothing in the nativity stories can be taken as true according to those who are learned in the liberalizing of our faith. The census was probably a literary device to get the principal characters to Bethlehem to fulfil the supposed prophecy in the Old Testament. Certainly there was no virgin birth — Jesus, presumably, must have been conceived out of wedlock and the offspring of an unscrupulous carpenter and a foolish village maid. Probably there was no stable, but certainly there were no shepherds, no angels singing the praise of God, no star, no wise men, no flight into Egypt and no massacre of the innocents. These are all treated as legends which have become encrusted around the coming of Jesus into the world. Of course He only came into the world as we all come into the world — there is no Incarnation. Like many of the gnostics in the early centuries of the church, many 'modern' thinkers consider it absurd to talk of God becoming a man.

The whole of the public ministry of Jesus is treated in the same cavalier fashion. In His life there were few, if any, miracles; certainly no changing water into wine, no walking on water, no feeding of thousands with a few pieces of bread and fish, and there was no raising of anyone from the dead. His miracles were really dramatic parables, His teaching the collective wisdom of the early church and, as with all the Bible, I must not simply believe the Gospels as if they were factually true. So I have been assured that He did not claim to be the Messiah or the Son of God, and that if He did, then this is due to a misunderstanding of His role and the wrong use of words. It all seems so clever but, I suspect, it really is *imaginatively* clever.

It is admitted, as far as I know, by everyone, that He died on a cross but the resurrection has been removed from the realm of fact to some mythological sphere where it is truth precisely because it did not happen. The claim of the risen Christ that, 'All power is given unto me' was never really uttered because, at the time He was supposed to be proclaiming that proposition His bones were rotting in an unmarked grave in Palestine.

All this work of literary destruction has, strange to say, been carried out in the name of Christ and truth. It has been considered that the Jesus of faith must be replaced by the Jesus of history so that our faith may be strengthened. I have been assured that this will give Jesus His proper place in our world and our affections. He is the man for others, the living embodiment of love, the perfect man.

I must confess real doubts as to whether the Gospels should be treated in such a surgical fashion. The fact that the writers did not write biographies in the modern manner does not prove that they have no biographical details. It is a common complaint by incompetent critics that writers did not produce an entirely different type of book, but such comments are unfair and foolish. Then the fact that the Gospel writers used source material seems to me to be a respectable thing for any historian; I find it hard to conceive of anyone recording history — either past or contemporary — and not using original sources. Lest someone thinks they can catch a glimpse of a chink in my armour, let me assert that I do not see that this invalidates inspiration.

The crucial question is simply whether, in the Gospels, we have a true account of the historical Jesus, and the main arguments against such a thesis are either literary or theological. As I suspect the whole basis of the liberal theology, it requires no detailed arguments against their criticism of the Gospels. But as someone who has a great respect for literature, perhaps I should consider their literary critique of the Gospels.

Honesty compels me to confess that I am not an expert in the art of literary criticism, but even within my limited knowledge I suspect that those who ruthlessly submit the Gospels to literary criticism are not so expert either. Certainly I know none of their works where they apply their literary theories to other works of literature. Perhaps I would really have to respect their scholarship if they showed the same insights and applied the same penetrating critique to the works of Chaucer, Marlowe, Milton or even Ian Fleming.

I may be forgiven for letting my sense of the ridiculous take over in considering what would happen to the plays of Shakespeare if they were submitted to the indignities which have been heaped upon the Gospels. Many theories spring to mind which could be presented as the 'assured results of modern scholarship'.

It would be taken as obvious that no one man could have written all the plays and sonnets and a careful study of the text would show various hands and influences. It would then be suggested that although some early fragments (a dramatic Q) seemed genuine, most of the material was of a later source. So it would be taken as reasonable to suggest that, as the myth of the Elizabethan era grew, so stories, epics, poems, jokes, characters and rumours abounded and some unknown redactor collected them under the name of William Shakespeare. It would then be proposed that we should study the works of Shakespeare, not to see the works of an Elizabethan dramatist, but to understand the corporate myth about Elizabethan England which later arose.

Of course, I take it to be self-evident that biblical critics, turning their attention to Shakespeare, would be in the Baconian school on the question of their authorship. They would be more interested in the myth than the man and would have some really radical suggestions to make. In a play, such as *Hamlet*, which contains drama, pathos, action, psychology, humour, introspection and exuberance, it would be taken as a fact that it was not the production of one man. So a new documentary hypothesis would be developed showing that it was really the work of Marlowe, Raleigh, Jonson, Donne and the brother of Shakespeare's mother, known as Uncle Tom Cobbleigh!

However, it is probably unfair to criticize works which have not yet appeared, but I will be more than interested when I find these literary critics turning from the Bible to apply their wild theories to the wide world of general literature. Meanwhile I will continue to suspect their methods and conclusions in their approach to the Gospels.

As I understand it, their basic arguments against the real historicity of the Gospels must be found on the theory that the writers did not really record what they saw and heard. It is said that stories about Jesus, fragments of His life and teaching, were widely circulated throughout the early church and these were collected to form the Gospels. If, as Luke claims to have done, these stories were examined, researched and verified, then I could have no valid criticism against the theory. But it goes much further than that: it is said that the early church developed its doctrine and even wrote stories about Jesus to illustrate their theology. So, rather than giving a factual account of the life and teaching of Jesus, the Gospels are really theological myths that were constructed to suit the theology of the early church.

I suppose I should now find myself in a conflict of loyalty: whom do I believe — Luke, who was a member of the early church and had met the eyewitnesses of the doings and sayings of Jesus, or the modern theological literary critics who can see myths and legends in everything? As a simple Christian, I see no guilt in believing Luke rather than men nineteen centuries later telling me he was wrong.

If the Gospels are carefully and cleverly contrived myths which are powerful and relevant — even though mythological — then I find Peter categorically denying such an assertion. He writes, 'We did not follow cleverly devised myths when we made known to you the power and coming of our Lord Jesus Christ, but were eyewitnesses to his majesty' (RSV). Perhaps I will be forgiven for accepting the testimony of Peter, who was there, instead of that of contemporary scholars who arrogantly look back over the centuries, peering into the ancient documents with humanistically-coloured spectacles and announcing their findings. It may be scepticism, but I find it hard to believe modern scholars who seem to claim that they know more about what happened in the first century than those who were actually there.

Paul certainly took it for granted that those who were there knew what was going on. On trial and giving his defence, Paul was interrupted by Festus, who thought he was mad to be talking about such irrational things as a man rising from the dead. Paul asserted, 'I am not mad. . . the king knows of these things. . . this thing was not done in a corner. . . ' To Paul it was common knowledge because the life, death and resurrection of Jesus did not take place in a corner. Now I have those who tell me it did not take place at all or, if it did, then it was in an existential realm beyond history and fact. It was a mythical event which took place in a mythical corner. Perhaps if Paul could hear some of the arguments which are now being used he would, like Festus, begin to wonder who exactly was mad!

Pick your own Jesus

Of course I am fully aware that it is only the most radical of theologians who are prepared to scrap almost every page of the works of poor Matthew, Mark, Luke and John. But the effect of their critique has permeated most biblical scholarship so that the Gospels, rather than being read for their content and challenge, are often approached as if they were not completely trustworthy. We are back in the old 'pick and choose' theology. Men turn to the Gospels, read about Jesus, and then decide what to believe and what to discard in the light of their own theories and presuppositions. Although it may seem simplistic, I take the Gospels to be the same as the Bible — it is either all or nothing; I suspect that to take part and reject the rest is to find the whole edifice in danger of collapsing around our ears.

So there are those who suspect the miracles, are unhappy about the claims for the divinity of Christ, but suggest that these questions pale into insignificance compared to the ethical Jesus. It is His moral teaching that is important; and the sermon on the mount is hailed as the prime example of the ethical Jesus. It may be presumption on my part, but I must confess that when people say such things I find myself wondering if they have ever read the sermon on the mount. After all, in this sermon, Christ claims to have come to fulfil the prophets and, even more startling, to be Judge of all the world, by saying, "Many will say to me in that day, Lord, Lord, have we not prophesied in thy name? And in thy name have cast out devils? And in thy name done many wonderful works? And then I will profess unto them, I never knew you; depart from me, ye that work iniquity.'

In all the teaching of Jesus the same holds true: intermingled with the noblest of moral concepts are the most astonishing claims. He claimed to have been before Abraham, to have come from the Father, to be one with the Father and to have authority to forgive sins. He was the incarnate God and the only real alternatives to that are that He was either mistaken or a liar. The escape route of asserting that He did not say certain things is a cheap and unacademic debating trick. All we can know of the earthly life of Jesus is found in the four Gospels and a few references in the Epistles. If it is decided what kind of a Jesus is wanted, and that only those parts of the Gospels that agree with that view are acceptable, then what is being done is done on the principle that if the evidence contradicts the theory then the evidence is wrong! Can I be blamed for seeing this approach as neither academic nor intellectual?

What really confuses me about this selective approach to the life of Jesus is that I am never sure how the principle of selection is made. If the writers were mistaken about the virgin birth, miracles and claims for deity, how do we know they were not also mistaken about the moral teaching and love of Jesus? It is the same Gospels that tell us about both. It may be cynicism, but in any book where I had to discard anything from fifty to ninety per cent as misleading or false, then I would be more than suspicious about what remained.

Of course, modern man may not be prepared to accept the Gospel record but this is no new phenomenon; many Jews and Gentiles rejected it at the time. The truth is not made any more palatable by being removed into the realms of myth, legend or existential history. So, being physically unable to eat my cake and at the same time still have it, I take it to be reasonable to believe that the events of the Gospels are either true or false history, and it is only in our sad and confused age that any other possible position could even be considered.

Behind all the theorizing and discussion on the historical Jesus and the truthfulness of the Gospel records, I sense a deep-rooted loss of nerve and fear in the twentieth century. It seems to spring from a dread of confronting modern man with the real truth — that in spite of his advances and achievements, his true state is such that he requires God to come to his rescue. Man, even modern man, is a sinner before God and only God Himself can save.

Of course, this theorizing is also an easy way of avoiding real questions, as I have experienced. Some years ago, at a theological conference, I shared a room with a man much learned in the ways of modern liberal theology and, as we talked long into the night, we came round to the subject of the resurrection. He waxed eloquent on the existential reality of the resurrection, asserting that it was not primarily a historical event but something for 'now'. Indeed, like a liturgical incantation he kept joyously proclaiming that 'Resurrection is now.'

I asked him if Jesus had actually risen from the dead, and was treated to a further dissertation on the meaning of the resurrection, which had nothing to do with an empty tomb, but was concerned with the victorious myth of ever dying and ever living. I repeated my question, asking if the man Jesus, being dead and buried, had actually risen from the dead, and again I was treated to a short lecture on the importance of the existential reality of life from death. Indeed, I could only keep repeating my simple, yet to me, important question, and after many digressions and much theological side-tracking, he ended by accusing me of asking the wrong questions!

To assert that the question is wrong is certainly a comfortable way of avoiding the need to provide answers or commitment. If the new apologetics mean proclaiming that we have the answer, providing people ask the right questions, then they do not really appeal to me and, I suspect, will not gain a great hearing in the world of men.

So the question of the physical resurrection of Jesus is, to me, not only valid, but crucial. From my reading of the New Testament, I understand it was equally crucial for the early church and on being challenged and mocked they did not take refuge in reducing it to an emotional, existential or mythical truth; they claimed to be eyewitnesses or to be able to produce eyewitnesses and evidence that Christ had risen. They were prepared to support the assertion of the resurrection by pointing, as Paul did in 1 Corinthians 15, to Scripture, the apostles and up to five hundred witnesses and, finally, their own experience.

It is no surprise to me that many deny or find it hard to

accept that a man, dead and buried, could arise and walk about, talk and even eat a meal with his friends; but the fact that it is hard to accept is not a valid reason for denial. What is often forgotten in our discussions of the scepticism of modern man is that the Gospels show that the disciples acted in exactly the same way as modern doubting man. They did not believe the resurrection at first, dismissing it as something ghostly, old wives' tales or simple hallucinations.

Jesus, on many occasions, had foretold that He would rise from the dead but, after the crucifixion, the disciples forgot His words; His enemies did not forget. So it was the authorities who arranged for a guard on the tomb while the disciples fled in fear and terror. They showed no evidence of expecting the resurrection.

Then when Mary and the other women found the tomb to be empty, they did not realize that He had risen but assumed that someone had stolen the body. Even when some of the disciples saw the risen Lord they still did not believe it, thinking they were seeing a ghost. Jesus had to say to them, 'Behold my hands and my feet, that it is I myself; handle me and see, for a spirit hath not flesh and bones as ye see me have' (Luke 24:39). Even then they still found it beyond their comprehension and, to prove the reality of His resurrection, we read that He then ate some fish with them.

That same night two of the disciples were on the road to Emmaus when the risen, unrecognized Lord joined them and, in telling Him of the events in Jerusalem, they ended their account with the words: 'Now certain women say he is risen.' So, having been told of the resurrection, they had simply refused to believe it, taking it to be an old wives' tale, and had set off for home. Of course, there is also the well-known incident with Thomas, who appeared to be an early logical positivist in demanding empirical evidence to have the resurrection verified.

So the Gospel records do not show the disciples as simple, credulous men and women who, with their primitive minds, were all too ready to accept the miraculous. In fact they acted like contemporary men and women. But they were

compelled, by seeing the evidence to accept the brute fact —
Jesus had literally risen from the dead. He was alive and the
tomb was empty.

If there was no resurrection, then I am not only believing a
lie, but have no hope in this world or the next. It may be
against the norms of secular experience or the closed universe
of the rationalists but, as a Christian, I can find no answer to
the challenge Paul threw out to Agrippa: 'Why should it be
thought a thing incredible with you, that God should raise
the dead?' So, unashamedly and simply, I believe God raised
Jesus from the dead and this actually happened in real
history.

It seems to me that to take the plain account of the
Gospels and turn it into something symbolic and imaginative
which never actually occurred is to indulge in literary vandalism. Even to make it a non-physical event is to mean that it
did not actually happen. I must confess that such interpretations are beyond my mental powers and must remain in the
province of those double-thinkers who see words as not
meaning what they mean and treat biblical evidence with the
respect normally given to fairy tales.

To my mind, untutored though it may be, to remove the
resurrection from factual history is to be overwhelmed with
demanding and real unanswerable questions. In my discussion
with the friend learned in liberal theology, I was accused of
concentrating on the historical rather than the existential.
But my position is that I can know the existential reality of
the risen Christ because He historically arose and I know Him
to be alive today.

I may claim to have a valid and existential experience of
Christ today, but if the resurrection did not take place, how
can I know the validity of my experience? Is it only through
emotion, imagination, intuition or mere sensory sensations?
In the final analysis, my religious experience may be self-
deception or even a mental aberration. But if Christ is risen,
then I can claim my existential experience is based on the
fact that He who was alive and was dead arose at a particular
time and place in history and is alive for evermore.

'Now is Christ risen,' thunders Paul and believing it to be the Word of God, I believe and accept. The modern alternative, 'Now is Christ risen. . . spiritually. . . mythologically. . . symbolically. . . existentially. . . ' is unacceptable to my simple faith and deepest understanding. If the Christ of the Gospels did not do miracles, reveal God, rise from the dead, then I, for one, find it very hard to rejoice in the mighty non-acts of God.

The Jesus of factual faith

Label me as a fundamentalist, a literalist, a simpleton, or whatever description springs to mind, but I believe in the Jesus of the Gospel records. Where else can I find out about His life, teaching, love and sacrifice? Where else can I get to know Him? The same documents which tell me of His gracious teaching and compassionate love also tell of His miracles, and the same writers who write of his death record the resurrection. It is there for me to read and understand. So I read it, not as mystic events which can only be understood as poetry, myth, music or sacred drama, but as a record of facts.

So, instead of complaining about the theories and imaginative ideas of those who would corrupt and confuse my understanding of Jesus, let me tell something of the Jesus I know and trust. He is the Lord of the Scriptures, both the Old and New Testaments; He is real, was historical and is now contemporary; He is the answer to all my sins and all my problems.

He is the One foretold by the Law and the Prophets and, through His Spirit, He is able to show me in all the Scriptures the things concerning Himself. It was on the instruction of the angel that He was named Jesus, because He would save His people from their sins and, although only a few shepherds welcomed Him on earth, all the choirs of heaven sang praises to God at the sight of the Incarnation. He was a man and yet truly divine, God made flesh. He went about doing good, healing the sick, raising the dead, forgiving sins, and such was

His power that even the winds and the waves obeyed Him; all the time He was showing and telling the way to God.

Because men love darkness rather than light, they plotted to destroy Him and eventually murdered the Lord of glory. But He was not a helpless victim, a hero dying for a cause, a freedom fighter or an innocent suffering under an oppressive regime: He was the Lamb of God bearing away the sin of the world. So no man took His life from Him; He laid it down of Himself — the Good Shepherd giving His life for the sheep. Twelve legions of angels were ready, waiting and willing to come to His aid, but they were never called. He who knew no sin was made sin for us to bring us to God. Of course, as the Giver of all life, death could not hold Him and He was raised by the mighty power of God and is alive for evermore.

All power, all authority in heaven and earth was then delivered into His hands and He is Lord and King over all. He reigns now and, although I do not yet see all things put under His feet, I know that the day will come when every knee will bow and every tongue confess that Jesus Christ is Lord.

Even such a brief outline will doubtless appear childishly simple to the keenly academic minds of those of the liberal theology and it will be considered that my views belong to the realms of immature fancies and childish dreams. But, even though it may hurt my pride in my intellectual abilities, I must confess that I have no faith in a fallen mind which, through sin, distorts the truth of God. The Jesus revealed in the Word of God is enough for me. So I see no conflict in the Jesus of faith and the Jesus of history; my faith is in the historical Jesus revealed in God's inerrant Word.

Apart from all the academic arguments there is one fact which has always appealed to me. The simple story of the nativity, miracles, deeds, words, death and resurrection of Jesus has inspired the greatest art in painting, music, poetry and literature. I have yet to see the art of the new Jesus who was not born in a stable, did no miracles, and died to be gone for ever. Where is the triumphant music in praise of the mere man who was the collective product of the church? Where are the hymns and prayers and poems in adoration of the 'man for others', the man who thought he was God and died a criminal?

I find it interesting, and perhaps significant, that liberal theology has not produced a liberal hymnbook. Perhaps my suspicions are right — only the Jesus Christ of the Scriptures can teach men how to sing.

Down by the riverside

I was sitting on the riverbank far from the noise of the town and only the song of a distant lark disturbed the silence. An open Bible was on my lap and I was reading Isaiah.

Suddenly I was no longer alone. A man stood towering above me, obviously a learned man; the lines of profound thought were engraved on his brow and he had the slightly vacant look of the scholar.

'Do you understand what you are reading?' he asked in a voice both cultured and authoritative.

'Yes,' I replied, going on to explain that before reading I had prayed for illumination, claiming the promise of the Holy Spirit. Before I had finished my explanation he interrupted with a torrent of words.

'You must understand that "enlightenment by the Holy Spirit" is a primitive concept which can have no valid relevance to real theological inquiry. In fact it is setting up a dichotomy between intuition and reason. Today, in our approach to ancient documents which are generally classified as the Bible, we have more scientific and theological tools at our disposal than the pietistic fundamentalism which negates reason and is essentially anti-intellectual.'

I tried to tell him that I understood the phrase to mean that reason, which was God-given, should be subject to the Holy Spirit, but as he was in full vocal flight I doubt if he heard my voice. 'Yes, today there is a full range of academic tools we can bring to the Bible. There are science and philosophy, literary criticism and the new historicity, rationalism

53

and existentialism, and all the assured findings of modern scholarship. So, without being caught in the Cartesian dichotomy, we can see how the dialectic tension can be embraced, rather than resolved, by the technique of a Hegelian synthesis. The current development of existential thought has opened the way for a true evaluation of the mythological base of our faith, enabling us to discard the old concepts of rational causality and traditional historicity. Added to this we have the Darwinian hypothesis which, treated as a fact, can add new dimensions to the search for becoming and being, as well as giving new directions to the search for meaning. Truth is contained in the mythological symbolism which is found in the imaginative history of the Bible and can only come to light through the application of the scientific method. Now do you understand?'

I tore my eyes away from his hypnotic gaze and looked down at the words in my Bible and for a moment I had the strange sensation that the river was giggling and the distant lark was hooting with laughter. Slowly I raised my head, but he had disappeared. The sun still shone. I went back to the words of Isaiah.

4
The Holy Spirit—I believe in the Holy Spirit

God is one and yet God is three-in-one; this, as I understand it, has always been the orthodox Christian position — there is God the Father, God the Son and God the Holy Spirit. As a simple Bible believer I accept the reality of the Trinity, even though as a small and finite being, I find it far beyond my rational comprehension. But I see no problem in accepting as true many things which are beyond my understanding. For instance, I would not deny the reality of electricity, radio, telephones, television, computers and the innumerable objects of contemporary life which are outwith my understanding. Of course, for those who see the flaw in my argument, I must make plain that I do not accept the doctrine on the grounds of empirical evidence. I believe in the Trinity because God has revealed Himself as such in His Word.

So I believe in the Holy Spirit. Yet it does seem to be a fact that modern theological scholars — particularly those anxious to escape from what they call the 'dead orthodoxy' of the past — neglect, or have no doctrine of, the Holy Spirit. Much has been written about God the Father — though perhaps 'Father' is too simplistic a word for those who like to think of themselves as wise — and there are many books on Jesus, though they often present a different Saviour from the one presented in the Gospels. But books, learned articles and lectures on the person and work of the Holy Spirit do seem to be few and far between. He is the neglected member of the Trinity.

Now I am fully aware that there are theological reasons

why this should be so; the office of the Holy Spirit, according to Scripture, is self-effacing. It is He who convicts men of sin, opening their eyes to their need and turning their hearts to Jesus Christ who alone is Saviour and Lord. The Spirit of God does not draw attention to Himself or intrude on His own behalf, but works in the hearts and souls of men to bring submission to Christ and worship to God the Father.

But in modern liberal theology I suspect that the silence about the person and work of the Holy Spirit is more than just an appreciation of His self-effacing role. While we can learn much about a man's theology by his books, lectures and the things he says, it is also true that we can learn a great deal about what someone believes by the things he does not say and the areas which he ignores. The neglect of the place and purpose of the Holy Spirit seems to me to be tantamount to a denial of His existence. The truth of the matter is that the Holy Spirit does not, and cannot, fit into the current thought patterns and man-centred ideas of the age.

Yet the Scriptures have taught us that the Holy Spirit is the Third Person of the Trinity. He is involved in the creation of life and all the gifts that men have; He is the primary Author of Scripture and is able to illumine the words to our understanding; and it is He who convicts us of sin, converting our hearts, regenerating our lives and sanctifying us, that we might be true children of God and faithful servants of our Lord. He is able to lead us into all truth.

The Giver of life and gifts

Perhaps I will be accused of having a one-track mind, but it seems to me that all our Christian beliefs must be affected by our attitude to the Bible. Only the rock of truth can provide a real foundation for a valid theological system which will grow and develop, each piece fitting neatly together, and be able to withstand all storms and criticism and the fierce winds of mockery. If the Bible is seen as merely academic sand then any structure superimposed upon it will ever be in danger of collapse. So, without apology, I confess my understanding of the person and work of the Holy Spirit is based upon Scripture and not upon the theories and ideas of men.

I read that the Holy Spirit is involved in creation. At the very beginning of the Bible it is recorded that, 'The Spirit of God moved upon the face of the water.' Then when God made man He breathed into his nostrils the breath of life or, as Job puts it, 'The Spirit of God hath made me and the breath of the Almighty hath given me life' (Job 33:4).

While I may, in simple faith, accept this as true and truth, I know full well that it is not in accord with modern 'scientific' thought. It personalizes creation, making the world and human life the actual creational work of a divine Person. The concept that the infinite may be involved in creation is acceptable to modern secularized thought, but only on the contradictory proviso that it should be understandable within the terms of finite science. In other words, the doctrine of creation is recognized provided that God worked as a Newtonian mechanic, an Einsteinian physicist or a Darwinian biologist.

Alternatively, creation is removed to a mythological 'reality' where all questions can be evaded, all problems avoided, and all debate reduced to a literary discussion on the meaning of poetic terminology. All things are acceptable and permissible as long as they keep God far away and long ago. But the God of the Bible is infinite and personal, and the Holy Spirit is shown as a Person who creates and sustains life; it is in Him we live and move and have our being. He is not Nietzsche's 'will to power', a Shavian 'life force', a Darwinian 'evolutionary spirit' or a mystical creative urge; He is the Third Person of the Trinity, the Holy Spirit.

Not only are we dependent upon the Holy Spirit for the gift of life itself, but He is the source of all the gifts which all men have; all have come from His hand. I have an uncomfortable suspicion that this may be too humbling a concept for modern arrogant man to accept uncritically. As a child of this age, and a child of Adam, I know something of how difficult it is to accept that all my talents and abilities, my mental and physical capabilities, are all gifts from God and are not the achievements of my own hands. It is the Spirit of God who gives all gifts and talents.

I take it to be significant that the first time we read in the Bible of a man being 'filled with the Spirit of God' is in Exodus 31 in connection with the building of the tabernacle. God, the Holy Spirit, enabled Bezaleel to design and create the artistic decoration of the tabernacle. He was not only given wisdom, knowledge and understanding, but the practical abilities of workmanship and craftsmanship to carry out the task to which he was called. Other men, too, were given gifts to help in the work. So it is made plain that the ability of these men as artists and craftsmen was given to them through the medium of the Holy Spirit; their gifts were not of their own making.

The idea of the Spirit bestowing gifts on men is carried throughout the whole Bible; all that men have and can do, all spiritual, academic, artistic or physical skills have been given through and by the Holy Spirit of God. Indeed, I know that through His common grace God has given gifts to all the children of men, to the good and the bad, the evil and the righteous — all manner of gifts to all manner of men.

Such a view of men's abilities as gifts crushes out all human pride, as well I know from my own heart. If I have any ability, any gift, it is glorious to my sinful heart to hear praise and have congratulations heaped upon my head; it is humbling to realize that by myself I have nothing but what was bestowed upon me by the Spirit of God, who gives gifts according to His perfect will. So it is with humility I must confess that I can appreciate why this aspect of the Spirit's work is not so generally recognized in the modern world. There is no room for academic arrogance or self-satisfaction. The gifts have been given to bring glory to the Giver and not to make the recipient proud of his abilities; all things are meant to bring glory to Almighty God.

Of course, there are a diversity of gifts, and among them are the gifts of wisdom and understanding — the very things which are used by those who would deny the authority of Scripture and question every doctrine in creeds and confessions. It is a sad fact that, in a fallen world, sinful men can twist and reverse the very gifts of God and use them to serve their own ends or another idol. Even the rich gifts of wisdom and understanding can be used for evil ends — as all those who live in the twentieth century well know.

The Guide to wisdom and truth

It was Jesus who promised the gift of the Spirit to His own disciples, promising the Counsellor who would teach all things and be the Guide into all truth. The Spirit of God is the gift of God through Christ to all Christians, to be their guide into all wisdom and truth.

Perhaps it is cynical to repeat the assertion, but I must confess that I have failed to see much evidence of a humble dependence upon the Spirit of God in many works of modern theology. In seeking to instruct me in the things of God many of these books and papers overwhelm me with the weight of human wisdom and the cleverness of the human mind. So often theories and concepts are presented as if the ultimate authority for all knowledge is human reason. Or, as is so true today when reason and rationalism have failed to explain the mystery of life and creation, the arguments are presented as if existential reality were the ultimate basis for truth. Everything becomes relative and even authority becomes merely a matter of academic opinion.

Some may be foolish enough to believe that I am now re-treating into a form of pious anti-intellectualism. Such is not the case. But I believe, and I have scriptural authority for the belief, that it is the fear of God that is the beginning of wisdom, and not purely academic study and the mastering of various subjects and disciplines. Certainly knowledge and information must be acquired through disciplined study, which is a valid activity commanded by God, but true wisdom is to be found in living before His face in fear and faith. It means recognizing our utter dependence on Him, submitting ourselves humbly to His Spirit to lead us into all truth. Such an approach to the problems of our age and to the dilemma of man is not widely welcomed by a generation that has been told that 'Man has come of age,' and has been encouraged to see itself as wiser and more learned than any previous generation. Only a schizophrenic mind can function with an awareness of its utter dependence upon God and yet be proud of its own capabilities.

All this leads to what seems to me to be a crucial question. If the Spirit of God is to lead us into all truth, how do we know the truthfulness of the things He brings to our minds? As I read from the teachers who are seeking to illumine the faith to me in the contemporary world, how do I know the things they say are true and of the Spirit? Must I turn to the scholars of the ages to see if the fresh insights are true? Do I accept them if they agree with the Socratic search for universals or the Platonic concept of reality? Is it because they illumine, in a fresh way, the Aristotelian 'golden mean' or are in accordance with the Cartesian world-view, Hume's scepticism, Kant's 'Copernican revolution' or the categorical imperative? Or is it Kierkegaard's 'leap of faith' or the various branches of existentialism from Heidegger, Sartre or Camus, or even the early or late Wittgenstein? Let me confess that in my simplicity I do not turn to these men, even though I know of them and recognize that they have much to say and much to teach me. I turn to the Bible.

If the Spirit is guiding us into all truth, then it must follow that He would reveal nothing contradictory to the Word of God which is truth. After all, it is the Spirit of God who is the Author of the words of the Bible; all Scripture is 'God-breathed' and men wrote as they were moved by the Holy Spirit. Jesus Himself claimed this to be true when he said, 'David himself said by the Holy Spirit. . . ' (Mark 12:36). So, even in the light of modern scholarship, I would assent to the proclamation of our Lord that 'The Scripture cannot be broken' (John 10:35).

But today in many circles the Bible is treated merely as an interesting collection of ancient documents, perhaps worthy of respect but neither infallible nor inerrant. This really means that there is no final authority and nothing by which I can measure the insights which I may believe the Spirit is giving to me. If the Holy Spirit had anything to do with the Bible of modern liberal theology then it was to produce a book full of errors, contradictions, misunderstandings and misleading statements. Such a book must provide a very flickering light and an unreliable lamp for the paths of life.

It seems to me to be more truly rational and true to my existential experience to accept the Bible as truth and allow the Spirit to be the Guide to the words He has written. I know something of the Holy Spirit through the Scriptures and can understand the Scriptures through the Holy Spirit. If I seem to be arguing in a circle, then I must assert that in logic all arguments are circular; the premiss always appears in the conclusion and the conclusion contains the premiss.

This leads to a basic concept which is often ignored today. Although this is not popularly accepted, either in academic circles or among the masses of ordinary people, an understanding and appreciation of God's truth is not automatically available to all men. This seems plain from Scripture. The god of this world has blinded the eyes of them that refuse to believe. It seems to me that this explains why there is so much theological and even cultural confusion in our age: the blind are trying to lead the blind.

If we seek to evade our dependence upon God and deny the illumination of the Holy Spirit, how far can we trust our own knowledge and understanding? Here, as in so much else in the Christian faith, there is no room for human pride. The biblical view is plain: we are sinners, born in sin and shaped in iniquity. But the very concept of original sin is now considered discredited and not worthy of serious thought. Yet, the orthodox Christian faith has always taught that not only is sin in the world and in the heart of man, but that it affects every facet of human life and behaviour. It has even infected our minds and understanding.

So if Darwin could find himself wondering how he could trust a mind that came from the lower animals, how much more should Christians distrust the human mind and reasoning abilities that have been corrupted by the Fall? Certainly, through the goodness of God and His common grace, all divine light has not been extinguished, but the mind of man is not free from sin and error. It is in active and ceaseless rebellion against God. So Rousseau's concept of men being born free but everywhere in chains is theologically — and in terms of practical politics — naive. So is the romantic vision of Wordsworth seeing a baby coming into the world trailing clouds of glory. Man is born a sinner, chained and bound to be a slave to sin and the kingdom of darkness.

But there is hope as long as man does not put his trust in himself and his own capabilities. The Spirit of God has come to give us that hope.

He who calls and sanctifies

Perhaps it is too simple for superior minds, and too old-fashioned for modern theologians, but I believe that through the Spirit of God, the free grace of God the Father and the finished work of God the Son on Calvary, there is forgiveness, redemption and new life possible for all men. But sadly, in our age, even in Christian circles, there is a vagueness about the real questions of sin and redemption.

In liberal theology today there is a vague undercurrent of universalism; there is the idea that all men are the children of God, and all will eventually be brought into the kingdom by the all-forgiving Father. This doctrine finds artistic expression in a poem by the Irish writer, James Stephens, where he dreams how, at the end of all things, Satan and all the demons are welcomed back into heaven and all is forgiven and forgotten.

The idea that all men are on their way to heaven is certainly a comfortable and comforting doctrine. But I must confess that the question that haunts my mind is not how attractive the concept may be, but how true? It was Jesus who claimed that at the end of the age he would say to some of us, 'Depart from me, I never knew you.' Then I remember it was the same Jesus who said to the decent, respectable and no doubt intelligent, Nicodemus, 'You must be born again. . .

you must be born of the Spirit. . . ' Indeed, He made it an absolute; if we are not born of the Spirit then we will never see the kingdom of God.

Jesus was showing that one of the crucial functions of the Holy Spirit is to bring men and women to new life, to give a new birth, a conversion, regeneration and new creation. Just as the Holy Spirit is the Giver of natural life, so it is He who brings about the new life that is necessary for the Christian life. Of course I am aware of how simple and old-fashioned this must sound to those learned in the modern doctrines. If they ignore or deny the Holy Spirit, reducing Him to a vague cosmic impulse or an influence emanating from the 'divine' side of human nature, then it must follow that the Holy Spirit is not personally involved in our salvation. Yet the Scriptures claim that He is. This presents no great problem to the modern mind; all that is required is to doubt the text, discard the doctrine, reinterpret the theology and produce a new philosophy which is more in harmony with the desires of fallen man.

But in my simplicity I accept the text and the doctrine. I am a Christian, but like Paul I cannot be arrogant in such an assertion. I have been saved and born again through faith, and even that is not of myself; it is a gift of God, given through His Spirit. Such an experience is only the beginning of the Christian life, just as natural birth is a beginning rather than a complete fulfilling. After the new birth we are called to walk worthy of the Lord, to be holy and perfect as He is holy and perfect. Indeed, we are called to serve Him in all things, even eating and drinking to His glory.

To resort to theological language, which may itself be 'old-fashioned', we are to be sanctified and again, according to Scripture, this can only be achieved through the work of the Holy Spirit. Perhaps it reveals the limitation of my reading, but I suspect that this is an area of the Christian life that is much neglected by those learned in liberal and modern theology. The idea of sanctification is ignored, treated as something mystical, an experiential sensation of the 'wholly other' or it is reduced to social work in the community or the political sphere of human experience. The word 'holy' has become associated with pietism or puritanism, implying self-righteousness and hypocrisy; to use the word with such connotations is not only a gross slander on the Puritans, but also a misunderstanding of the need for sanctification.

However, we are called to be holy and sanctified, fit for the Master's use. These things can never be achieved in our own strength or by the exercise of our own wills, but they can be ours through submission to God and His Holy Spirit who will guide and help us to grow in grace and knowledge of the truth. It is the Holy Spirit who enables us to pray, sometimes in the agony of groans which cannot be expressed in words; then, when we are called to witness for our faith, He will teach us in that same hour the things we should say. By His grace He will enable us to sing in the dungeons of life, even at the desolate hour of midnight.

Perhaps I should not be surprised at the lack of consideration apparently given to the office, work and person of the Holy Spirit in the modern schools of liberal theology. Such a doctrine as the personal, infinite Third Person of the Trinity does not fit easily into the mould of the twentieth-century mind. Today man takes pride in his questing spirit, his ability to probe and dissect, sceptically approaching all things in his search for truth and God. Man is treated as if he were autonomous, master of his fate and captain of his own soul. Like Scripture I have a very high view of man; but I also have, through the same Scriptures, a realistic view. He is great — and he is a sinner, even in his mind and thinking.

So in my simplicity I see the Holy Spirit as searching everything, even the heart of man and the deep things of God. Without the Holy Spirit we are as nothing and can know nothing of the ways of truth or the reality of God. Without the Holy Spirit there is no possible way in which fallen man, living in a fallen world, can find the real way, the ultimate truth or the everlasting life. Sin has blinded the eyes of our understanding and so corrupted our minds that the truth is not in us and we love the darkness rather than the light. Darkness is no less black even if it is expressed in lofty concepts and philosophical language.

In spite of the Fall which alienated sinful man from a holy God, bringing death and eternal separation, the Holy Spirit draws men back to God where they are accepted through the blood of Christ — the one sacrifice for sin for ever. So men can be reborn into the kingdom of light and liberty, the kingdom of God where the Comforter and Counsellor will illumine the hearts and minds so that none need stumble or fall. I confess I feel no necessity to apologize for the simplicity of my theology, though I can understand those who want it changed and modified to suit the current world-view of the age or the latest fads of contemporary theology. I stand by the things which have been taught me in the Scriptures.

In our Lord's own words, the Holy Spirit comes to testify of Him. But as so many of the learned in our century want a Jesus made to suit the detailed specifications of secularized, humanized man, perhaps I should not be surprised that they reject the Jesus revealed by the Holy Spirit in the Scriptures. It is almost self-evident that the Jesus of modern scholarship, the man for others, the freedom fighter, the noblest example, all differ radically from the testimony of the Holy Spirit to Jesus the Saviour of men. To quote one obvious example, John, writing through the Holy Spirit, tells us that the *Logos* was God, became flesh and dwelt among us; now some modern scholars assure us in a recent publication that what we have is *The Myth of God Incarnate*. I find it hard to accept this as the Holy Spirit testifying of Jesus in our modern age, if He is contradicting all that He has taught for centuries.

In describing the function of the Holy Spirit our Lord went on to say that He would bear witness to sin, righteousness and judgement to come. Even to list these three things is to see how far they are removed from the teaching and doctrines of those who would hold to a more 'modern' and liberal theology.

Sin has been explained away and is no longer seen as a positive, fierce and destructive force in the heart of man. It is taken as part of his finitehood or part of his old Darwinian nature which is slowly being evolved out of his system. The idea that sin is total rebellion against a just and holy God, leading to total separation from Him, is considered somewhat old-fashioned, and the idea that badness is just the absence of goodness holds more appeal to modern man. Such a view of sin is certainly not that revealed by the Holy Spirit in the Scriptures.

Righteousness has been redefined until it has ceased to have any meaning and has been emptied of all meaningful content. Indeed it has been reduced to 'love' — a word beloved by modern liberal theologians as they can make it mean anything they want to make it mean and it can even cover a multitude of sins. Love is that which we do according to the situation; the only absolute is love and love itself is not an absolute! Righteousness, right living, is treated as a concept, not a call for dedication and commitment; it is being taught today in many different guises from that revealed by the Holy Spirit in Scripture.

The concept of the Spirit's bearing witness to judgement is, of course, quietly ignored today. It is an uncomfortable doctrine which modern man tries not to think about, and the easiest way is to treat it as a primitive theory which has no place in contemporary study. Yet Jesus said the Spirit will bear witness of judgement, and heaven and earth may pass away, but His Word will stand for ever. Judgement is not the condemnation of our own consciences or the feeling of failure which all men know; judgement, as revealed by the Holy Spirit in Scripture, will be judgement by God. This, naturally, is an unpopular doctrine, but our authority should not be our own hopes or the popularity of our views. It is truth that matters.

If human reason is placed on the throne, then it is not surprising that the Holy Spirit must be relegated to being merely a historical doctrine that has no relevance to the modern world of thought; or if everything is reduced to the existential reality, then there is no place for the Holy Spirit of God. We then reach the position where He has nothing to teach us about the real world of the twentieth century and if, as I suspect, this is the view of modern theologians, then it is not surprising that theology is in a complete muddle and only adds to the confusion of a post-Christian culture. We end in the 'abomination of desolation' as spoken of by the prophet Daniel!

However, I believe in the Holy Spirit, the Third Person of the Trinity, who is able to lead me into all truth. If such a simple belief must be discarded before I can become a mature Christian in the contemporary scene, then unashamedly I want to remain a child, holding on to my Father God, because I believe that it is only the Holy Spirit who can bring me to the fulness of manhood in Christ Jesus.

Yes, I believe in the Holy Spirit.

Nightmare
A hymn to truth

Concept of truth, we cannot know
Just what you are, or who —
But this we know, the Bible is
The truth which is not true.

So we may soar with Kierkegaard,
Or Tillich's mind so keen,
And learn the uselessness of words
From Ludwig Wittgenstein.

Teach us, Hegel and Heidegger,
Pascal, Camus and Sartre;
And may our minds for ever learn
From Bultmann, Brunner, Barth,

Bonhoeffer and Martin Buber,
Whitehead, John Stuart Mill,
With Nietzsche, Niebuhr and Moltmann,
All servants of thy will.

We praise the world that Darwin made,
Big Bang that made the sun;
For gifts of Huxley, Wells and Hoyle,
True humanists every one.

Great spirit of the latest truth,
Forgive both Greek and Jew
For those far off, forgotten days,
When truth was seen as true.

Now as mankind has come of age,
And leaves the days of youth,
We know the Scriptures are not true,
And know them to be truth!

Ah! Men!

5
Truth—I believe in truth

'What is truth?' asked Pilate, not recognizing the truth when it was staring him in the face. He then walked away without waiting for a reply. No doubt, like many of our modern thinkers, he believed that such a question was simply unanswerable and beyond the wit of mere man.

What is truth? In the contemporary situation it sounds such an old-fashioned question that I should hesitate to raise it. Yet to the simple rationality of my mind it is the crucial question around which all discussion and debate must centre. Study, dialogue and debate are all in vain if there is no truth at which we can arrive; all search and experiment become aimless and every consideration and academic pursuit becomes an end in itself. The search then is made to be the whole purpose rather than a progress.

Of course, the concept of truth is not being ignored or denied completely, but I must confess that the silver cords of my sanity are being tangled beyond belief when I consider how it is being treated in my generation. Truth is being removed from the realm of fact into the sphere of fantasy; it has been relegated to a mere matter of opinion, a psychological experience, or simply the expression of a prejudice. It has been taken up into the highest reaches of philosophical speculation where it can only be expressed in the most technical and academic of language. Others, to my further bewilderment, assert that it cannot be expressed at all but must be accepted with silence. In an intellectual Babel all voices must be equal, and not only are all things up for question, but all answers must be denied. Indeed we are in the remarkable situation where, if I claim to know and believe the truth, then I lay myself open to charges of dogmatism and intolerance.

So truth has become more elusive than the needle in the haystack. But even though many thinkers no longer believe in the existence of the needle, they are still joyously plunging into the hay; after all it is less dangerous to work purely with the hay — needles can be painfully sharp. So the search in the haystack continues in the hope of avoiding the needle of truth for if it was found then they would have to accept it and submit to it.

The truth that is not true

As I understand it, in the development of modern secular philosophy, truth has increasingly disappeared from the realm of reality. Descartes, the father of modern philosophy, tried on the basis of pure rationalism to prove that no idea should be accepted as true which is not distinctly and clearly beyond doubt. He then put his method into practice and showed that it was possible to doubt everything — except that he was doubting. So *Cogito, ergo sum* — I think, therefore I am. But, having shown that it was possible to doubt everything, he was really unable to put certainty back into the things he had doubted.

David Hume refined the element of doubt into pure scepticism which revealed that in the final analysis we can be really sure of nothing, not even of ourselves; we must be sceptical about all conclusions which come through the use of reason, sense perception or experience. In spite of all the efforts of other philosophers, these seeds of doubt have been buried deep into the thought of Western philosophy and neither Kant and the Continental philosophers, nor the British empiricists, have been able to put the truth, like Humpty-Dumpty, together again.

Then into the turbulent waters Freud threw a stone which the modern sons of Enlightenment are still trying to ignore, or by embracing are finding themselves sinking without hope.

Freud showed that man is not a coldly rational creature, capable of unbiased judgement or objective thought, but is a being governed by dark impulses and strong forces which he can neither control nor fully understand. In view of this, it became almost a symptom of pathological, or psychological disorder to suggest that we can know the objective truth. What then becomes important is why a man believes what he does, and not whether it is true or false.

Perhaps I should confess that I have suffered from this approach. Many friends, with a more liberal theology that I hold, have often been perturbed about the affliction of 'fundamentalism' from which I seem to suffer. When they find out that I was brought up in an evangelical home by parents who were simple Bible believers then their liberal heads nod wisely and a strange light enters their eyes. The mystery has been solved and they can understand my insistence on an inerrant and infallible Bible; it was all a matter of social conditioning and parental influence that made me a fundamentalist. The crucial, and to me blatantly obvious, question as to the truth of my position becomes irrelevant to them. It seems to be a victory of Freud over common sense.

What makes such accusations more painful to bear is the fact that I realize that these same people would be insulted if I dared to suggest that their opposition to my theology is all a matter of social conditioning and parental influences. Yet on their own terms such an argument would be intellectually valid. They are liberal in theology because they were conditioned so to be, or as is so often the case, they have rejected conservative evangelicalism because they are rebelling against their upbringing. But such arguments do not appeal to me, being in themselves a denial of the truth.

So in the modern situation truth seems to have all but vanished from the scene. The analystical philosophers have tried to catalogue all statements into meaningful and meaningless categories so that only those which could be verified could be considered valid and true. Their theory seemed to provide a measuring stick for truth and had the added bonus of abolishing all the troublesome metaphysical questions about God, eternity, morality and all the other things which have haunted the heart of man. Unfortunately, in abolishing metaphysics, it not only threw overboard philosophy but, as the critique of Karl Popper showed, ended by discarding science and making scientific statements 'meaningless'. Ultimately, of course, logical positivism failed for the simple reason that it could not verify its own 'verification principle'!

As the Bible teaches, and as I believe, it is in the heart of man to seek to avoid being confronted with the truth and many other means of doing so are now being pursued. The linguistic school, under the Wittgenstein cult, have found that by concentrating on the language they could forget the question. By focusing all their attention on the words themselves, their meaning and how they are used, whether they are facets of reality or distortions, they could happily forget the need to find any answers. Within such a philosophical school all questions and problems about truth become mere confusions of language.

Then there is the growing influence of existentialism — both the secular and sacred varieties. Man is seen as being trapped in existence in an alien universe where there is no meaning and life and truth must be absurd. But man can authenticate his own existence by rebelling, choosing or making a leap of faith in the dark. Truth again vanishes into a maze of assertions and experiences but cannot be held to be objectively there.

If anyone fears that I have forgotten my primary aim of making a reasonable confession of faith and showing how I cannot commit the folly of denying God's Word, this brief excursion into secular philosophy is not without relevance. It seems to me that if I would understand modern liberal theology I should not turn to the Bible but to the secular philosophers. It is they who have had the greatest influence on the new thinkers of theology, and not the inspired writers of Scripture. Too many Christian scholars, rather than out-thinking the worldly philosophers, have blindly followed them, to the confusion of the simple Christians and the bewilderment of the faithful.

The end result of this modern theology and biblical criticism seems to me to be a greater confusion than that found in the ranks of the Philistines. As I understand it, what they say about truth is so complex and complicated that it affects my mind in the same way as the mind-blowing drugs do that of the addict. Yet their position seems to be quite simple: it is just that the truth is not true.

So my problem in believing the Bible today is the uncomfortable fact that the most radical and daring teachers of the Bible today are quite happy to assert that the Bible is truth. In their books, papers and lectures, they point to the Bible with an apparently sincere and passionate honesty and proclaim, 'Here is truth.' But when, in the simplicity of my approach to truth, I try to understand what they mean, I find a great chasm yawning between us and I have the unpleasant sensation of having no ground beneath my feet and of my mind performing endless somersaults. They believe that truth is not true.

I have been assured that the first three chapters of Genesis are truth — inspired, eternal truth, but they did not happen! Indeed, imprinted on my memory is one occasion when I feared that the hinges of my sanity would give way under the shock, as a Christian appeared on television to tell us all that the creation account in the Bible is truth precisely because it did not happen. As if that was not enough, he went on to assert that if it had happened as recorded in Genesis then it would not have been truth!

Needless to add, it is not only the first three chapters of Genesis which suffer from this approach; this is now being presented as if it were the only way to understand the Bible. So we find treated in the same way Abraham and Sodom and Gomorrah, Joseph and his jealous brothers, Moses and the Red Sea, Elijah on Mount Carmel, Daniel in the lions' den, Jonah and the large fish and many, if not all, of the miracles in the New Testament. They are truth and they did not happen. Equally the virgin birth and the resurrection of Jesus must be taken as enshrining truth, but on no account must they be taken as true in the way that most people of sense would take the word.

Perhaps I should make it clear that I am not totally naive, nor concerned purely with scoring cheap debating points. I am fully aware that there is such a thing as poetic and artistic truth. I know and fully appreciate that the fictitiousness of a poem, novel or play in no way invalidates the truth it may contain or reveal. The Greeks knew the value of myths and fictionized drama long, long ago; but what really perturbs me is the way modern scholars are developing the theories of mythological truth in ways that are, if not beyond the wit of mortal man, at least beyond the understanding of this poor, simple soul. They seem to be happiest when everything can be reduced to a myth.

Mythological truth

In my less lucid moments I sometimes wonder if the greatest myth of our age is the myth about myths. History and all of life can only be understood in terms of myth. Learned men write about the myth of creation, the myth of the Fall, the myth of redemption, the myth of resurrection and the eschatological myths. I once heard a Christian priest talk profoundly about the 'myth of nature' and the 'myth of life' and found myself wondering if, at a funeral, he ever meditates on the 'myth of death'. Reality and truth seem to be in danger of being lost in the mists of a new mythology and truth can only be seen if it is non-factual.

The problem for these learned gentlemen is that, like a man on the mountainside who has a lisp, they are seeing everything through a haze of myth. Perhaps they talk to their wives about the myth of love, marriage and sex; to their children about the myth of the family and parenthood, and meditate on the myth of crime and violence increasing all around them. Mere mortals, like myself, are compelled to live in a real world where real things happen to real people at real moments of time.

This is how I can understand my Bible. I do not find it

written as a collection of myths and legends but as understandable historical events; only the 'myth of modern
theology' could see it otherwise. When I read of creation and
miracles the words of Abraham echo in my ear: 'Is anything
too hard for the Lord?'

Of course, men can refuse to believe the facts of history;
today many believe that Che Guevara still lives and that
Hitler or Bormann did not die in 1945, but we cannot turn
these events into a myth. To take biblical accounts of events,
written as history, and turn them into a myth is to deny the
Word of God. It is, obviously, as many humanists recognize
with suspicion, a cheap way of trying to have the cake of
Christian truth without choking on eating the unpopular fact
of a God who acts in history.

In accepting the Bible as the Word of God written,
infallible and inerrant, I believe it has its own unity and
completeness. If one part is reduced to a myth then the other
parts are in danger of disappearing into the same realm of
myth. I feel it is debasing to my manhood and an insult to
my rationality to proclaim publicly that my faith is firmly
rooted in a myth. So I hold to the whole Bible as being true
within its literary structures, and maintain that to take what
is written as history to be myth is to put other parts of the
Scriptures at risk.

There is the obvious example of Jonah and the great fish.
Few, if any, modern liberal theologians would accept the
book of Jonah as a historical account of real events. They
would say it is to be seen as a myth, a parable, or simply a
good short story revealing a strong vein of Jewish humour
and a moral. Many arguments are no doubt brought against
the historicity of Jonah: no fish could swallow a man; a city
could not repent in such a short time, or God would not act
in that way. Jonah is comfortably placed among the myths
which enshrine truth; it is truth without being true.

When we turn to the New Testament it is to find the uncomfortable fact that Jesus accepted the adventures of Jonah
to be truth and to be true. He said that the people of Nineveh
repented and were more worthy than those of His own

generation; indeed on the last day they would be raised up in judgement on His own wicked and perverse generation. Now it may be the lack of 'mythological spectacles' but I cannot see how I can avoid the conclusion that Jesus understood the book of Jonah to be an account of actual historical events. It seems to me almost idiotic to accuse people of not being as good as characters in a mythological story. Neither does it promise real or fair justice when we are told that we will be condemned because we did not respond to God's message in the same way as the characters in a short story.

I am fully aware that such arguments will not silence those who start with the assumption that because it is in the Bible it may be truth, but cannot be true. They probably have an endless variety of explanations: Jesus was wrong; He misled his hearers; He did not say those words at all, or He was just not as clever and theologically learned as we are. But, if any of these explanations are correct, then once more I am left wondering how I can believe anything else He said. I still hold to all or nothing.

Myths do have a place in human life, but when everything is seen as myth, then reality is crushed out and it is truth that becomes the casualty. Truth must be related to fact. Even secular philosophers, who have largely given up the search, generally concede that truth must be related to something outside of itself. So even the truth that is revealed in myths must have a relationship to facts or else it is merely a matter of opinion. The arts and myths can only illumine the truth, not create it; but much modern theological thinking seems to delight in removing the concept of truth from fact into a mythical realm where the human mind can twist and shape it to suit the patterns of the age and the desires of the human heart. This is why it is an irrational age and an academic sin to be dogmatic and an intellectual iniquity to be certain of holding the truth. Facts are often uncomfortable things, interfering with our theories and not quite fitting our myths.

So it is not surprising that even facts are being challenged. If truth belongs to a never-never land then facts will not fit into the mythical landscape. I am assured that the Bible is not about facts, but about an interpretation of facts, and the profoundness of this statement is supposed to silence me. Indeed I have been told more than once that there is no such thing as a fact; there is only an interpretation of a fact. It must be confessed that such a proposition leaves me in the confused state of not being sure whether to laugh or cry.

When I was born my parents gave me the name John — that, to my simple understanding, is a fact and I cannot see how it can possibly be considered an interpretation. It seems perfectly logical and reasonable to say that the Battle of Hastings was fought in 1066, and the Battle of Waterloo in 1815, and to assert that these are facts and not interpretations. Perhaps I should add that I do know and accept that all historical writing must include selection and interpretation, but to make sense these must be based on facts. To assert that the facts are dependent upon the interpretation seems to be turning logic on its head.

This is why I have a great deal of sympathy with Dr Johnson's simplistic argument against the idealist philosophy which asserted that everything was spirit and therefore material reality was an illusion. He kicked a stone and said, 'It's there and that's an end to it.' As far as he was concerned, anyone who did not believe in the physical universe should kick a stone and see if the result confirmed their theory. Facts, like stones, are there and it is folly to imagine otherwise.

I would hold it to be a philosophical and theological necessity for truth to be based on facts and, something which is often denied today, that there is such a thing as truth. After all, if there is no ultimate truth, then not only are debate and discussion pointless, but the differences cannot be resolved; any form of relativity in the concept of truth must only lead to confusion. Only a geographical idiot would suggest that all roads lead to the same destination and I suspect that if those who believe that all things are true were to put their theories into practice when going anywhere they would end where many are today — lost.

So, in my simplicity, I believe in the truth which is true,

not in relativity where if all things are true then nothing is true. Neither do I believe in a pragmatic truth where, if it works, if it helps, then it must be true; in a fallen world it must often appear that the practical and best thing is to believe a lie.

I believe that truth is found in fact, not in fairy stories, and the truth of God is revealed in the Bible, not in the mythology which men delight in imposing upon it. Having lived among men all my life, knowing them and knowing my own heart, I find it hard to accept what mortal man claims to be the truth. It is to God that I must turn to learn of the truth, believing that He would not deceive me with lies, cleverly devised tales and the truth that is not true. I see it as no cause for shame that I should publicly confess that I would rather believe the words of God than the words of men.

What is truth?

But, as Pilate asked, 'What is truth?' He did not really want an answer, just as today many, enjoying the search, do not want the answer either, because to find the answer, to find truth, must mean obedience, submission and commitment, and these are things the sinful heart of man does not want. Like Adam, they want to be as gods.

In all humility I can claim to know the truth. I have found the source of truth which is spiritually satisfying, academically acceptable and does not offend my intellectual integrity. I know Jesus Christ to be the truth and I know Him, not only through my existential experience, but through the Word of God written. As He Himself said of the Scriptures, 'They are they which testify of me.'

I am conscious that many are more than unhappy about the way my arguments always return to the Bible, and I have been accused of believing in verbal propositions rather than a person. The gospel, they tell me, is Christ, not the Bible. I must confess a complete inability to separate the two because it is from the Bible I first learned of Jesus and it is to the

Bible I continue to return in order to learn more of Him.

Perhaps it is the essential simplicity of my approach and understanding, but when I believe in a person I also believe his words and the things he says. So I believe in God and therefore must believe His Word; I believe in Jesus Christ and must believe the words He has spoken and the Scriptures which are all about Him. So, rather than having faith in propositions and not in the Person, my position is that the propositions are about the Person.

The simple Bible-believing position seems to be infinitely more reasonable than the complicated additions, divisions and subtractions of those who multiply theories to explain all of life as well as the ways of God with man. Their answers and concepts of truth are often beyond my understanding because they are so busy condemning the specks in my eye that they never notice the planks of inconsistencies that are embedded in their eyes.

'Where is the wise?' asks Paul and, perhaps it is cynicism, but I am often tempted to answer the rhetorical question by suggesting they are not to be found in the divinity colleges and universities of our land. Yet perhaps they are, because Paul continues, 'Has not God made foolish the things of this world?'

Accepting God's truth means that we will be foolish in the eyes of this world. If to believe the truth of the Bible and the truth personified in Christ is foolish, then I confess to being a fool. Perhaps I should add folly to foolishness by spelling out the extent of my simplicity.

I believe the Bible is truth and true. I believe God made the world — *ex nihilo*; perhaps this seems foolishness in an age of evolutionary dogmatism, the many schools of neo-Darwinists, concepts of Big Bang, Steady State and Oscillating theories. It does not seem to me to be incredible or illogical to believe God made the universe out of nothing. I have seen the heavens which declare His glory and the earth which shows something of His handiwork.

Then, perhaps more astonishing to my liberal friends, let me reiterate that I believe in the literal truth of Adam, Eve and a Garden of Eden. I believe in a real historical Fall; not only do I read of it in the Bible but I am, in the twentieth century, surrounded by the evidence of a fallen world.

As I take it to be self-evident that nothing is too hard for the Lord, I have no difficulty in accepting the miraculous or the fact that God can make a bush burn without being consumed, part a great sea, bring water out of a rock, or even make an axehead float. I do not think it foolishness to accept the Incarnation, believe that God can make a virgin conceive or, as Man, can walk on water, raise the dead and command the wind and the waves to obey Him.

I am sadly aware that many will pity my condition and see me as one of the last relics of the old breed of fundamentalists. They will consider that I am not only out of touch with the modern world, but hopelessly out of date, probably having read nothing that was written later than when the last of the Puritans roamed the earth. What worries me about such a judgement is that it is reducing me to a myth and not a man. The truth is that I have lived in the contemporary world and know from first-hand experience something of the agony and perplexity of life in the twentieth century.

In this age of McLuhan I have sat before the electric media listening to and watching the pundits of our global village telling me everything — except what is truth. I have, being still a Gutenburg Man, read the works of Marx, Freud, Jung and ploughed through the philosophy of Russell, Ayer and even the words of Wittgenstein and the Huxley brothers — both the Aldous and Julian variety. As my friends know, my bookshelves bear witness to my reading of Kafka, Joyce, Orwell, Lawrence of Arabia as well as the Lawrence of the mining towns, Sartre, Camus and other secular prophets of my century. But, even though they had much to teach me, in none of them did I find truth or the ultimate answer.

I know what it is to sit in the theatre with Becket, waiting hopelessly for a Godot who does not come. Let me confess I have been bored by Brecht, puzzled by Pinter, infuriated and dazzled by the logical absurdities of Ionesco, and enraged by the torrents of Osborne or the socialistic diatribes of the 7.84

Company. Again, though I learned some things of value, there was no truth on which to base my faith and to which to commit my heart.

Art has always had an appeal for me. So in sad and bewildered contemplation I have stood before canvasses created by Picasso, Matisse, Dali, Bacon, Pollock, Warhol and the whole range of cubist, expressionist, abstract, pop. op, surrealist and all the schools and movements of the twentieth century. Many of them pierced my heart and opened my eyes, but they could not give me a faith for which to live and die; they could not supply the truth.

The more I studied, the more intense became my search, the greater became the conviction that it was the Bible, the old-fashioned book of my fathers, which alone contained the truth — which was true. I came to realize that it must take a very special type of mind to see people as Darwinian specimens, evolutionary accidents, naked apes or unprogrammed computers. I did not have that type of mind and could only pray that it never would be mine; I wanted to see people as people, created in the image of God and loved by God. Then it was obvious to me that the scientific optimism of the old-fashioned humanists could only be a sick joke in an age of hydrogen bombs, biological engineering, ecological crises and pollution. Marxism and all the political philosophies spawned in our modern world offered no real hope to my heart.

Equally, as this confession shows, the twists and turns, irrationality and flights of fancy of the modern liberal theologians could not satisfy my search for truth. They could only add to my confusion. I seemed totally incapable of believing that a historical lie could be a religious truth and that I would find truth by accepting myths, legends, stories and fables as the way God would speak to rational man. Even though I could not claim to be a literary scholar I was aware of the vast gulf between the works of Homer and the books of the Bible. I could not equate Aesop with Moses as producing the same literary genre or believe that the brothers Grimm were in the same business as John and Paul.

So I turned to the Bible and accepted it with the simplicity of faith, finding the answer to the very things which perplexed me and knowing it to be true and truth. Many will consider this to be a confession of foolishness rather than a confession of faith but it is the position on which I unashamedly stand. I believe the Bible, but it is the Bible as it is written, not the truncated version that is left when the modern scholars have finished with their cavalier criticism and weapons of destruction. It is the Bible as written, inspired and trustworthy, that shows me the truth and that which is true. And I believe in Jesus the Word of God incarnate, the truth personified.

If such statements are dismissed as mere dogmatism, narrow-minded bigotry, sheer ignorance or arrogance, then I can make no apology. It matters little what anyone thinks of me, the real challenge is to face the fact that it is ultimately with God that I have to deal and it is what He thinks of me that will settle my eternal destiny. Surely no one can imagine a God who would condemn me because I dared to trust Him and His words rather than the opinions and theories of men?

Truth alone is in Him. It is that truth which I accept.

Nightmare
The just shall live by doubt

As it should be written, 'The just shall live by doubt.'

And what more can I say? For time would fail me to tell of Voltaire and Thomas Paine; of Hume and Darwin, and of Huxley also; and of all the theologians who, through doubt, created havoc in the kingdom of the faithful and stopped the mouths of their critics. By doubt they quenched the fires of truth, made weak those who were strong, and turned to flight the armies of the simple believers. By doubt they revived from the dead ancient heresies and brought to life again the lies of a distant past.

They have been published, fêted, made famous and applauded by great audiences, appearing on the media to earn great renown (of whom this world is worthy).

All these made sure they received a good report, being skilled in the arts of publicity. And they give us the promise that, if we too learn to doubt, we may like them come to the fulness of contemporary manhood whereby we may doubt all things. Seeing therefore we are encompassed about with so great a cloud of doubters, let us lay aside every weight of faith and suspicion of belief, and follow after them to where we might believe in nothing.

6
Faith—I believe

I have often been told, indeed so often that I sometimes grow weary of the assertion, that this is not an age of faith. Once upon a time — and it is treated as if it was in the dim and distant past — there was an age of faith, a time when men actually believed and their faith affected everything they knew and did. But such an age is gone, relegated to the footnotes of history. While historians may repeat themselves, history does not, and faith has faded finally from the face of the earth. This, I have been assured, is an age of doubt.

It does seem to be so. The new intellectual starting-point for so much modern theology would seem to be Descartes's method, with a different conclusion. Today it seems to be 'I doubt, therefore I believe.' Doubt is presented as the great goal of the faithful, something more to be desired than a strong faith. Books expressing doubt on every doctrine are proliferating like the frogs in the Egyptian plague. God is doubted; His Word is doubted; Jesus is doubted; the Holy Spirit is doubted; all the creeds and confessions of the historic church are doubted. All is doubted, doubted utterly.

It is not simply in the academic sphere of lectures, learned articles and textbooks that these doubts are raised; even the media join in the game. Someone may proclaim the 'old, old story' of the conservative evangelical gospel, but such a thing will be greeted with a thunderous silence, for faith does not make news. But let someone, somewhere, bring forward a theory that Jesus was really a woman in disguise, a mythical personification of an early Marxist cell, or even the code name for a mushroom, then the headlines will proclaim the glad doubts and great publicity will be given to this new breakthrough in uncertainty. Trendy Christians will appear on television, perhaps in the usual carefully balanced panel where every possible viewpoint is represented except simple Bible-believing Christianity, and the new doubts will attain academic status and televised authority. It is never enough for them to express their own doubts, but they must ceaselessly stir up new ones until the grey dust of doubt lies over everything.

Simple faith has almost become something of which to be ashamed, the mark of ignorance and the 'closed mind'. It is treated as little more than a romantic belief, a sentimental escape from the challenge and accomplishments of the twentieth century, and a sympton of being completely out of touch with contemporary reality. Faith is seen as the new opiate for the immature because in an age when 'man has come of age' it can be discarded like the old coat the child has outgrown. Today, in our scientific, technological age, there is no room and no need for faith. It is, I am endlessly assured, an age in which faith has become redundant.

My doubts about doubt

Although in another context many are prepared to question the reality of 'facts', it is a strange paradox that whenever I mention 'faith', it is 'facts' that are used to bludgeon faith into submission. Facts have replaced faith. All around, I am told, are facts, scientifically proven facts, governed by the absolutes of logic and philosophical proofs of rationalism and existential authenticity. So, when we come to religion and questions of faith, doubt is the only approach.

Like everyone else in our culture, I have been affected by the atomic fall-out of doubt but (and this appeals to my sense of the ironic) I find myself with doubts about the doubters and their doubts. Of course, this may prove that I have been a good pupil because I want to go further than my teachers in doubting their doubts and questioning their questions.

The word 'doubt' simply means 'being in two minds' and I find it hard to accept this as an intelligent position to hold; it means we just do not know what to believe. Perhaps it is human pride, but I would feel somewhat ashamed to proclaim publicly that, when it comes to issues of God and man, life and death, I am not only in two minds but I just do not know what I believe and I want everyone else to be like me.

Then, in my simplicity, I often find myself wondering if indeed it is an age of non-faith? Rather than a generation dedicated to facts and proof, I suspect that we have the age-old mixture of fact and fancy, credulity and superstition, and it is not hard to suggest empirical evidence for such a generalization. I can point to the salesmen of our culture and the advertisements that appear daily in our newspapers and are screened hourly on television. I only need to listen to the promises of our politicians and see the worship afforded to the latest pop group. Then there is the revised interest in astrology and the occult, the search for pills to cure all our ills, and the new technological mysticism of the Von Dänikens of this world.

So when I am told that this is not an age of faith I have the strong impression that such a statement is only half a truth because it omits the latter half of the sentence. It is not an age of faith 'in God', and these are the words that are left out. The truth of the matter is that faith still exists, perhaps stronger than ever, but it has been transferred from God to science, sociology, education, evolution, reason, imagination, intuition or some other aspect of the creation.

But undoubtedly 'science' is the great opponent of 'faith' and I am expected to flee into the mystical realms of religion at the very sound of the battle-cry. Science and scientific proof must triumph over such a strange religious activity as simple faith. So on all sides my humble faith is assaulted by the facts of science and the assurance that faith has no place in the scientific enterprise. Pointing to the alleged facts of science, my critics assail me with the supposedly unanswerable question, 'Where is your faith now?' I am expected to remain in a defeated silence. Science is seen as the great arbiter of the facts and science alone is the objective search for truth unhindered by the ancient superstition of faith.

T.H. Huxley, the great biologist and publicist for Darwin, can be seen as the archetype of the true scientist; he claimed that his method was to sit before the facts and let them lead him, as a little child, to the truth. Such an enterprise has no need of faith — at least, so they assure me. It is the true scientist, sitting humbly before the true facts, letting them lead him to the truth. Let me confess that this picture does have its attractions and I must admire its shape and structure but, if I may hoist my critics with their own petard, it seems to me to have the elements of a romantic myth. It seems an excellent example of the scientific myth which now claims to be inerrant and infallible — though the source of inspiration may still be a matter of dispute.

To my simple mind this picture of Huxley sitting before the facts, without the imposition of faith, is a good illustration of an impossible man, sitting in an impossible position, attempting to do the impossible. It is not only psychologically impossible but philosophically absurd and theologically inconceivable. At least two crucial questions spring to my mind when I behold the vision of a Huxley before the 'facts'. Is there indeed no faith there? How truly objective is the whole exercise?

Whether he is aware of it or not, the man before the facts is exercising faith. He must have faith that he has got the facts, faith that he is capable of recognizing the facts, faith that he can interpret the facts and faith that there is order in the universe so that his findings can be applied to all similar facts. Indeed the very scientific activity is an expression of faith.

Then there is the question of how truly objective he is, as he sits before the facts. He sits there with a mind moulded and trained by his age; his whole outlook is coloured and focused by the moral and intellectual influences of his childhood and family. He brings to his study the fact that he is a child of his age and a product of his own culture. He brings to his researches his own philosophy, his own world-view —

indeed, his own faith. There is no way he can avoid looking at the 'facts' through eyes that are blinkered with his own prejudices and presuppositions.

In the case of Huxley there is no doubt that he embraced the faith of evolution, believing in something which could not be scientifically proved and certainly could not be duplicated in any laboratory. He was a man of faith, who put his faith into the way he interpreted certain facts, and these facts were chosen and understood to fit into his own faith.

In all the spheres of intellectual activity the same must hold true; faith is the root activity of man and no man can live without faith. The philosopher has faith in his reasoning powers and logic; the artist has faith in the ability to communicate; the educationalist has faith in the human capacity to assimilate information, and it could be argued, even if ironically, that even the nihilist has faith that there is nothing to believe in!

I must confess a genuine uncertainty as to where exactly the faith of the modern liberal theologian lies; their faith seems to depend upon what they are saying at any given time. So their faith moves from science to philosophy, or from intuition to imagination — indeed in many directions except to the place where God has spoken and revealed Himself.

So where I differ from those who do not hold to a Bible-believing faith is not on the existence of faith. They, too, in spite of their denials or qualifications, have faith. It is the object of their faith that I doubt and question. I doubt that science can truly explain all things and I cannot worship at the shrine of the 'scientific method' knowing that there are probably as many methods as there are scientists. I doubt that humanistic philosophy can ever answer all the real questions of life or that new theories of historicity will ever fully reveal the past. The concepts of new systems of education to overcome the Fall and create saints can only raise deep doubts in my heart. And certainly I have real doubts that human sociology will produce a perfect society or that new revolutionary theology, trusting Marx more than Jesus, will usher in the kingdom. Perhaps I should make clear that doubt is too weak a word to describe my attitude to all these things — denial would be more appropriate.

So I have real difficulties in accepting that I do not live in an age of faith. My complaint is that it is a time of great faith in anything but God. It is a time of cheap faith which, when analysed, is found to be in contradictory ideas and false philosophies. It is a new age of idols. Perhaps Doubt itself is one of the new idols we are all expected to fall down and worship.

God did not create us to become slaves of idols, no matter how academic they may seem, or make us to live out our lives in a continual spiral of uncertainty and doubt. We were made to believe and all men have the faculty of faith, but it must be rooted and grounded in God or else we will be led astray into the paths of danger and destruction.

I find it tragically sad that men will believe anything, except the Word of God, and will put their faith into anything, other than the living God. Modern man's life is full of 'certainties' — except when it comes to the things of God; from my reading I suspect that this is also true of the ranks of contemporary theologians — they are full of humanistic 'certainties' and religious doubts. I can only doubt the validity of their doubts.

A living faith

The Philippian jailer, seeing not only the prison, but his whole life and future lying in ruins around him, and with the hymns of praise from the dungeon still echoing in his ears, could only fall on his knees and cry, 'What must I do to be saved?'

As with so many questions in the Bible, this was not simply the agony of one man at one particular place, but the heart-throb of the human soul facing the ultimate questions of life. It was a cry for direction and meaning; a sob of anguish which still finds its echo in the heart of contemporary man as all his plans seem to turn to ashes and all his hopes are crushed by forces he can neither understand nor control. How can he be safe — saved?

The answer came immediately — Paul telling him that if he believed on the Lord Jesus Christ he would be saved. It was the great Pauline doctrine of justification by faith; it was faith that was the key to salvation for the poor, bewildered jailer, and for all those who are prepared to face the ultimate question.

In my simplicity I accept this glorious doctrine of being justified by faith. I can have peace with God and become a child of God. I cannot depend upon my own efforts or intentions, my good works or intelligence; all I need to do, all I can do, is hold out the empty hands of faith and accept the free gift of God in Christ Jesus. The Christian life begins with faith.

I am aware that this, baldly stated, seems curiously old-fashioned today. The very idea of a man publicly proclaiming that, 'If you believe you will be saved,' smacks of the early days of the Salvation Army and Victorian mission halls; it seems to belong to the days of primitive Methodism and the ultra-fundamentalists. But the problem is that the proclamation was made by the great apostle Paul; it cannot be written off as a simplistic and emotive doctrine that has no relevance to reality. Indeed it is not Paul's alone, but is written into the Bible from beginning to end.

But how is this doctrine of justification by faith treated today by those who would make the gospel more 'relevant for a technological age'? As someone who was born with a vivid imagination — sometimes a blessing, sometimes a curse — I delight to conjure up impossible situations and dream of how they would develop. But occasionally even my fevered imagination fails me. This is true when I try to picture what would have happened if, on rushing from the ruins of his prison, the Philippian jailer had met a gaggle of liberal theologians.

'What must I do to be saved?' the jailer would have asked, but then my mind whirls in contradictory circles as I try to recreate the events that would have followed. Rather than immediately answering, the theologians would have demanded to know what exactly he meant by 'being saved' and have quickly sought to disillusion him of primitive concepts of salvation. With great patience and learning they would have explained that he should not have let the earthquake upset him; it was a perfectly natural occurrence, completely in accordance with the infallible laws of nature, and should not be seen as any form of divine intervention. Of course, if the jailer had persisted with his question then the clever teachers would soon have found themselves in disagreement about the best form of treatment.

Some would have assured him that his desire for salvation was simply a realization of his finitehood and showed that he had not reached the depth of his being. Others would have suggested that, given his existential experience, it was a natural psychological reaction and it could easily be explained and treated. Again someone else would have been anxious to show the real philosophical problems raised by his question, assuring him that 'being saved' and 'justification' were word symbols and should not be taken as having content in themselves. So he would have been pointed to the depths of his being, to the eschatological hope of liberation, to the need to embrace secularization, or to — no, tragically my imagination is incapable of recreating the scene in all its richly comic possibilities. There is one thing of which I can be certain; they would not have answered with the words of Paul.

One picture does remain in my mind. It is of the Philippian jailer and his family, not being baptized, but being baffled. My sympathy is with him, and all those who, seeking salvation, turn to the 'clever' words of 'clever' men. Paul, in proclaiming the Word of God, had a real answer to a real need.

The Christian life begins with faith but, more than that, it is a life of faith. The just shall live by faith. By many, perhaps even by some of those in the evangelical camp, faith is treated as something mystical and belonging to the spiritual realm of life. It has little relevance to the real world of everyday living. But the Christian faith, and the faith of a

Christian, is more than the sugar on the pill of existence or a crutch to help us limp our way through life. It is not 'positive thinking' or a Sunday activity.

It is a trust in God in all things. It means daring to believe Him before the words of men, daring to claim His promises and rest our lives on His certainties. It is a living faith which affects all of life, so that all thoughts, words and actions are an expression of the faith we have in God. It is trusting God when the sun shines and trusting the same God when the storms break around our head.

'Though he slay me, yet will I trust him,' cried Job in agony and that was real faith. I can only read the words and realize that nothing on earth or in hell can defeat a man like that; he is triumphant.

Faith is to read the eleventh chapter of Hebrews and realize that it is speaking about real men and women who lived real lives in a real world. They are our examples, showing that it can be done, that we can trust God who loves us and in His grace is prepared to be our loving heavenly Father. Faith is to know that He is ever ready to hear our cry, listen to our prayers, give us His grace and strength and assure us that, if we are His, then all things will work out to His glory and our good.

Such a simple faith will doubtless be labelled 'reactionary' by those who rejoice in the fruits and findings of 'modern scholarship'. In the new liberal climate nothing must be sure or certain; not only must all things be open to question, but everything must be vague and unclear, and all theological affirmations must be so broad that they are capable of an infinity of interpretations. Where our fathers may have asserted, 'I believe. . . ' now we are expected to be intelligently profound by suggesting, 'I don't know if it can be said. . . ' It would appear that it is now theologically respectable to proclaim that 'Ignorance is bliss.'

I must confess that I find it irritatingly amusing that those who are most critical of my dogmatism, are often the very ones who are the most dogmatic. Ironically, they are men of great faith; but their faith is placed in human scholarship — in literary criticism, rational or irrational philosophy, or the great idol of the mythical 'scientific method'. They have faith in the demythologizers who claim to know more of what really happened in the first century than those who were there; they want me to have faith in progress, evolution, the ability of technological man to build a bigger and better Tower of Babel. They want me to base faith in a non-event such as the non-physical resurrection, to 'trust the future' with process theology or believe on the new gospel according to St Marx which teaches liberation through revolution.

No, I cannot walk with such men or follow their teachings. My faith is in God and, through His Holy Spirit, I believe on the Lord Jesus Christ. I seek, by His grace, to live by that faith in every sphere of life. There is no element of shame in this confession, as it seems to be more reasonable than all the wild theories and strange substitutes that have been offered to me.

A reasonable faith

The simple faith of the Bible-believing Christian is reasonable. Faith is certainly not, as the schoolboy howler puts it, 'believing something you know to be untrue'. Equally, I must confess, I am not completely happy with the more philosophical definition given by Thomas Locke who described faith as 'the assent of the mind to propositions which are probably, but not certainly, true'. If faith is only exercised in the areas of probabilities then it is in danger of becoming a matter of opinion. Rather than the God of the gaps — the God brought in to explain what cannot be scientifically understood, we have a faith of the gaps; faith exercised where we cannot know.

But faith, while it is much more, is also mental assent, yet in our confused and confusing age, even this seems to be doubtful. There are Christians who claim faith in the Creator, but do not assent to creation; faith in the resurrection, but they would not assent to it as an event; faith in the Bible, though they would not assent to its being true. Indeed my poor mind has scarcely recovered from seeing books, written by Christians, advocating Christian atheism. All this seems to me to show, not so much that they have separated faith from fact, but that they have confused sense with non-sense.

Even though it may appear simplistic to many eyes, I take it to be self-evident that it is reasonable to believe that there is a God. Then it certainly is a reasonable proposition, which the Bible itself makes, that to come to God one must believe that He exists. Regarding the question as to how we can know God, there is the fact that God made us creatures of verbal communication so there is no good reason why He should not communicate with us in verbal terms. Nor would He deliberately lead us astray, or His people astray for centuries, by mythological stories and historical lies.

To me, as a child of the twentieth century, it seems eminently reasonable to assume that man needs to be reborn and that the world is desperately in need of redemption and renewal. Any doubts on these propositions would soon be dispelled by a few brief glances at any daily newspaper or television news bulletin. Given the human condition, it does seem to me to be logical that God would do something about it; and the incarnation, death and resurrection of Jesus bear witness to the fact that God did indeed do something about it. He Himself was the Lamb, bearing away the sin of the world.

Then I take it to be reasonable to believe that if God created the world there must be design and purpose behind all things; God is working out His purpose and will fulfil His promises to make all things new. The Christ who came to Bethlehem will come again: He said He would and it does seem to me to be most unreasonable to claim to believe in Christ but refuse to believe the words which He spoke.

All these are items of faith which I take to be reasonable facts. Perhaps they are simple, but the truth is not necessarily complicated. However, I would hold it always to be reasonable. So it is faith in God, faith in the truth, that matters. I must confess what must seem an unchristian impatience with those who dare to tell me that it does not really matter what we believe because love and sincerity are the only criteria. But it is possible to be lovingly wrong and sincerely in error.

I had a friend who was sincere and loving, and one evening he was going to meet his fiancée in Glasgow. Being kept late at his work, he had to rush to the local station and only managed to jump aboard the train as it was leaving the platform. He sincerely believed he was on the right train and it was a journey of love because he was going to meet the girl he intended to marry. But sincerity and love were not enough; he was on the wrong train and the first stop was Perth. Faith, to be reasonable, must be related to the truth; it is never enough in itself.

So simple faith which trusts God and believes His Word is infinitely more sane and reasonable than the radical alternatives which are offered in the name of modern Christianity. The Kirkegaardian leap of faith does not seem a sensible thing to me; I would feel foolish inviting anyone to take a leap of faith in the dark to find the light. Rather than an invitation to a reasonable faith it sounds more like a plea to commit intellectual suicide. Equally being a citizen of a gambling-mad nation, I must hesitate before suggesting that people should make a Pascalian gamble in believing in God. There is nothing more unreasonable than betting. I want a reasonable faith. So to trust the ground of my being, embrace ultimate concern or trust the freedom of the future, where the kingdom will be ushered in by politics and revolution, are all irrational and unreasonable.

The faith that was once delivered to the saints is alone truly rational and reasonable. Why should I be ashamed to believe?

Nightmare
My soul, hope thou in—what?

Pulling the curtains, I sat in the darkened room giving myself up to the waves of despair that swept over me. It was deeper than despair; it was a sense of hopelessness. Outside my curtained windows I knew there lurked the reality of the twentieth century — weak governments, fading standards, growing anarchy and the vandals taking over.

'There is no hope,' I breathed the words, finding almost a masochistic satisfaction in their shape and sound. Then faintly, like the whisper of a summer breeze, words drifted into my mind: 'Hope thou in God,' but immediately other voices came, loud, arrogant, vibrating with the intensity of a strange conviction.

'Hope thou in the evolutionary process.'

'Hope thou in the eschatology of revolution.'

'Hope thou in the new age, struggling to be born.'

'Hope thou in the ultimate reality.'

Then the words came quicker, louder, merging into one another so that I could not tell if it was the sound of one voice or many, yet they echoed sharp and distinct in my mind.

'Hope thou in man. . . in mystic reality. . . in secularization . . . in progress. . . in science. . . in technology. . . in education . . . in the people. . . in the goodness at the heart of all men. . . in the death of God. . . in man's coming of age. . . in the theology of hope. . . in hope itself. . . in existential reality . . . in becoming and not being. . . in love. . . in sex. . . '

So it went on, voice upon voice, hope upon hope, until the

very air of the darkened room seemed to throb with the urgency of the voices. I crushed my hands over my ears, striving to shut out the babble of voices that were deafening me, but it was to no avail; they echoed louder within my throbbing head.

I tried to recall the words which had drifted into my mind before the onslaught of the voices, the words which had come with the refreshment of a summer breeze. But I could not recall them, they were gone.

There was only despair and the babbling screams of hope.

7
Hope—I hope

Not only is this a generation without hope, but strangely enough, they do not seem to miss such a loss. Certainly it is a fact that the mass man of the technological society functions better if he is conditioned by the mass media and purveyors of the pop culture to forget the absence of hope. So people have learned to try to forget what has gone and ignore what is yet to come. If they can eat, drink and be merry now, they see no need to regret the past or worry about the future.

The genuine artists of the age may strive to show the spiritual poverty of a one-dimensional and fragmented world, but they are just voices crying in the garbage dumps of the consumer society. Much more acceptable are the politicians, dangling the carrot of the ever-increasing gross national product and the trendy pundits promising a technological paradise. But even these are greeted with a healthy cynicism; the mass of people are too busy living in the present.

I suspect that this is equally true in the church. Hope is in short supply and the glorious promises of God which are yet to be fulfilled are not eagerly awaited with longing hearts. Yet once the church glowed with a burning hope. Christ would return and His kingdom be established with justice and righteousness. Such hope is to be found in the Bible and the writings of the saints down through the centuries. It can be heard in the plaintive melodies of the Negro spirituals and the triumphant hymns of Wesley who taught the people to sing. It was a hope in God. A hope that recognized that ultimately all things are in His hands; not just the onflow of history but each individual life was in the hollow of His hand.

What a glorious proclamation it sounds: 'I hope in God,' yet how curiously old-fashioned! Where is hope placed today?

Hope without hope

The advice of the psalmist, 'Hope thou in God,' is probably treated as too simplistic for contemporary man. Certainly I suspect it is too simplistic for the modern liberal theologian who would want to define hope and redefine God before considering the concept. He would then agree with the psalmist but in such a way and with such an interpretation that the Hebrew poet, or the ordinary man in the pew, could not have the faintest idea what he was talking about. Perhaps, in the sovereignty of God, this is all to the good.

But to simple souls such as myself, who want to cling to the promises of God and have their hope in Him, the 'old-fashioned' Bible is enough. It is here I find a strange and ironic paradox. I have no faith or hope in man by himself, to overcome his condition or solve his dilemma, and find that my views are echoed and defended by many of the secular thinkers of our day. It is the liberal theologians, who imagine themselves to be 'modern', who are old-fashioned and completely out of touch with the cultural and academic climate of the age.

Looking at the intellectual world of today, reading the cultural philosophers, social scientists, writers and artists, is to find a deep-rooted core of despair in all their works. The hopes and optimism of the last century have gone and the old concepts of human progress and advancement are treated with a great deal of suspicion and unease. So often I find myself wondering if it is not a fact that the most fervent defenders of evolutionary progress and hope in man are to be found, not among the ranks of the unbelievers, but in many who would claim to be 'modern' theologians.

Certainly there was a time when radical theology seemed to be in complete agreement with the cultural climate. Just when the theologians were getting into their stride of rewriting and reorganizing the Bible, Darwin came along to turn the whole scriptural revelation back to front. The paradise of the Garden of Eden was removed from the beginning to the end. Eden was not a long-ago historical place, but the end to which the evolutionary forces were directing man. As man was progressing, hope and optimism were the natural consequences.

Alongside this hope in the evolutionary progress of man came the growing awareness of the power of man. With science and technology there seemed to be no limit to what man could and would do in the world. Disease and drudgery would disappear; the monotony of work and physical effort would be banished, and men and women could spend their time developing their gifts and talents and pursuing their own interests. Such a view had the delightful elements of the romantic myth and we can read the vision in the early romances of Wells and the speeches of the politicians of the period. Men no longer needed to hope in God — that was the old idea of pie in the sky. Pies would soon be available on earth, as many as anyone could want in every conceivable flavour.

But in the mud-filled trenches of Flanders, and in the blood-stained heights of the Dardenelles, that hope began to be crushed out of the hearts of man and the first seeds of despair were taking root. Many began to wonder, as the poet T. S. Eliot did, whether mankind, rather than advancing to some future Utopia, were not 'advancing progressively backwards'.

Then the smell of burning hope could be experienced from the gas chambers of Nazi Germany and the polluted fall-out from Hiroshima. The second half of the twentieth century did not find bright faces lifted up to herald the new dawn; it saw heads bowed to hide the flow of tears from eyes that had seen the death of the great myth of progress and evolutionary advancement. The future became a 'brave new world' where Huxley portrayed the science that crushed the life out of individuality, and created, controlled and ruthlessly disposed of life. Or else it was to be an Orwellian nightmare of 1984.

Hope seemed to depart from the earth.

Evolutionary philosophy is dying for lack of evidence; the idea that mankind is getting wiser and better must be exceedingly difficult to sustain. To refute such a suggestion, it is only necessary to think seriously for a few minutes and face the questions that will arise in our minds. Have we really advanced and progressed and what do we mean by those terms? Have we better philosophers today than they had in ancient Athens? Do we care for our neighbours better than they did in Old Testament times, and is our behaviour towards one another an improvement on anything that has gone before? Certainly we do not stab, spear or painfully kill our enemies with sharp arrows, but that is because we have a more efficient method of annihilating millions with a push of a button.

We do not crowd to see public executions, but that is because we can sit in the comfort of our own fireside and see murder, rape, assault and various sexual activities in living colour on the television screen. For our added enjoyment and edification these can be instantly repeated in slow motion so that we can savour them to the full.

I confess a sly admiration for the mental capabilities of those liberal theologians who, in spite of all the evidence to the contrary, still hope in the evolutionary progress of man. I find it little short of astonishing that anyone born and living in the twentieth century can still hope in man, and it is no surprise to me to find that, at least in Europe which I know best, the intellectual climate in the post-war years has been one of pessimism rather than hope, despair rather than optimism. They see modern man waiting for Godot who, as everyone knows, will not come.

Equally I can only have an ironic admiration for those liberals who are old-fashioned enough to believe that the technological prowess of man will usher in the kingdom of heaven. Increasingly, technology is threatening man, making him a mere extension of the machine and reducing him to computer fodder. Rather than freeing him to fulfil his potential, technology seems to be taking over all of life so

that health, education, work, recreation, and the state and all
social organizations are functioning as machines rather than
the servants of man. Among the sensitive and intelligent of
our age many are expressing the fear that the machine, rather
than being a slave of man, is making man himself a slave.

Arthur Koestler tells the story of a Communist writers'
conference where there were endless hours of speeches about
the great new world in construction and the new transport
systems that could be expected in that world. Eventually,
André Malraux asked impatiently, 'And what about the man
who is run over by a tramcar?' But they were only interested
in the system, not in people as individuals, and the only
answer he was given was that in a perfect socialist transport
system there would not be any accidents.

Those liberal theologians who see in all this progress and
advancement a cause for optimism and hope can only be
whistling in the dark. It may be an admirable activity, but it
is still an essentially irrational one; it would be more sane and
reasonable to seek to light candles and show a more excellent
way.

In case I should be considered to be a new Luddite,
perhaps I should add that I am not against technology as
such, or even against the concept of some progress in
mankind's learning and abilities. It is the way these things
have developed in our godless age that is leading to all the
problems and adding to the human predicament of the
twentieth century. My position is quite plain. I have a high
regard for man, believing him to be one who bears the image
of God, gifted and capable, made to be lord of creation — but
a sinner. So my hope is not in man nor in the progress or
technology of man. That is the road to despair, a path of endless disappointments.

But, in spite of all the attempts to herd people into the
mass, to treat them as units and not people, to manipulate
them into a docile condition where bread and circuses now
are all that matter, people are still people. Just as man cannot
live by bread alone so he cannot live without hope. He is not
made to live in the narrow cell of the present or to see him-

self at home in the existential moment. So many are placing their hope in a new Messiah, Marx, as the one who will lead them into the promised land. Already this new messianic religion is holding sway over almost half the world where by the state all things consist and revisionists, rather than witches, are now being burned at the stake.

When the hopes of the old-fashioned liberal theologians seem to be crumbling to ashes, perhaps I should not be surprised that some are turning to the new hope of the world — Karl Marx. Revolution is now being given a theology all to itself.

I am aware that through the common grace of God all men have a knowledge of God in some measure and can have something to teach but, even accepting that, I must confess a sense of shock to find myself advised to consult Karl Marx as a biblical interpreter and see his works as commentaries on the Scriptures. But such is the case. Once Christians complained that the devil had all the best tunes; I find it somewhat confusing to be told that Christians do not even have the best theology.

Hope thou in Marx

In an age without hope we now have, by courtesy of those who find God's written revelation inadequate for the twentieth century, a 'theology of hope'. With the modern tendency to gild the literary lily it has been plastic-coated with many other adjectives: 'liberation theology', 'futuristic theology', 'revolutionary theology' and 'the theology of hope'.

Here again I must underline my introductory confession that I am not a trained theologian capable of giving a detailed critique of any theological system. In my simplicity, all I can do is give my impressions and doubts. As in so much liberal theology this new hope has succeeded in throwing my mental processes into such confusion that, like Alice in Wonderland, I am asked to shut my eyes and believe ten impossible things before breakfast.

These theologians of hope write a great deal about eschatology, claiming that all our understanding must be shaped
and moulded by it. Even though I lack formal education in
theology I do know that eschatology is concerned with the
'end things': with death, judgement, heaven and hell, and the
word has been used concerning the second coming of Jesus
Christ. But, as is obvious from the words of these writers, the
theology of hope is not concerned with the hope of the
return of the Lord. So, as Wittgenstein advised his students
not to ask for the meaning of a word but for its use, I find in
most modern theology words used in a completely different
sense from their traditional meaning. Indeed, just as modern
agnostic artists are now using Christian symbols to make non-
Christian statements, so I suspect that many liberal theologians are doing exactly the same thing with language. They
are taking the very words of Scripture and theology to mean
exactly and precisely what they want them to mean.

So eschatology seems, in the theology of hope, to be tied
to politics and revolution. It is an opening towards the
future, the 'glorious freedom' of the future. So they tell me
that the church should not be concerned with the past: only
the future matters; the past should only be of concern to
show how the future may be changed. But, what is even more
confusing to simple souls such as myself, they make the
assertion that even the present is unimportant; only as the
future grasps me can I have significance and realize the
messianic possibilities in man. The future means freedom.

Even more daring and, I suspect, more Marxist, is the claim
that the church may have to act as a revolutionary force in
establishing the future. This means that the Christian must be
prepared to stand alongside the terrorist, baptizing him with
a new Christian name, 'Freedom Fighter' and arming him,
not with the sword of the Spirit (which is the Word of God —
today considered an ineffective weapon!) but with the whole
armoury of modern technology — automatic weapons, rifles
and bombs.

This seems to me to be a delightful turn-round on the part
of those who are eager to condemn the conservative

evangelicals. During the Communist 'witch-hunt' of the McCarthy era in America and the protests over the Vietnam war, it was a common sneer that the white Anglo-Saxon Protestants were in a crusade for Christ against the Communists. The 'Bible-believing fundamentalists' were showing once again their intolerance and ruthlessness and this was satirized with the lapel button: 'Kill a Commie for Christ'. Now with the new theology of hope and liberation the Christians are called to be more compassionate and liberal and can 'kill a capitalist for Christ'. Perhaps it is the easy way out, but I suspect that neither slogan could be considered truly Christian.

Of course there is more, much more, in this new theology which sets alarm bells ringing in my mind and makes me fear for my sanity as I seek to understand it. The theologians seem to present a God who is trapped in sequential time — a proposition I had never imagined anyone could ever propose, as it seems to be a denial of the very word 'God'. But this new God they are seeking to reveal has 'the future as his essential nature'. He has not revealed what he has done or is doing, but what he 'will be and do in the future'.

So biblical events become irrelevant. Indeed they state that the resurrection is an irrelevant question if we want to know what happened to the physical body of Jesus. Once more my mind wings its way back to my liberal friend at the conference who accused me of asking the wrong questions and had all the answers to the questions I did not pose.

I cannot go along with this new brand of Christian Marxism which is seeking to bring hope back into a world which has lost hope. It is redemption, not revolution, that is needed. That redemption can only be found in Christ, and not in a new synthesis of Christ plus Marx, or Christ plus any political theory. Christians are certainly called to take part in a great struggle, but it is not against the forces of capitalism, reaction, or bourgeois standards, but against principalities and powers, against the spiritual rulers of the world system that is in rebellion against God.

As I am not an extreme pietist fleeing from all aspects of

the created order, I recognize that these spiritual powers often find expression in the political and social structures of a fallen world. Then we must stand against them, striving to redeem and reform through the grace and love of God. But our hope must never be firmly anchored in change that is purely political or social.

It is the poor who are blessed, and we are not told that they are to be blessed through overthrowing the rich and taking over their property. It is the meek who will inherit the earth and we are not told that they will come into their inheritance by an armed struggle to overthrow their oppressors. Men are meant to have liberty, equality and fraternity but these things will not come about through the mob in the streets, the bomb in the supermarket or banners on the barricades.

There may well be such a thing as a justifiable revolution, but an armed conflict will be no substitute for the redeeming power of the gospel. The kingdom will come, not through the efforts of men, but when the King comes and takes up the reins of power in the sight of all men. The very Word of God assures us that all will be accomplished, not by power, nor by might, but by His Spirit. It is here that our hope should be placed. Not in new and better theologies, not in the 'power of the workers' or the might of sociological ideas, but we should have a living hope in the living God. All other hopes are in a future built on shifting sand.

The gospel is liberating; it is a message of hope, and it is concerned with the future, but it is not man-centred, not an ideology, but a proclamation of truth. In Christ Jesus men can be liberated, and given a lively and living hope that will come to pass as the Lord has promised.

So, as I see it, this is an age of relativity — philosophical as well as scientific — and political pragmatism; a time of revolution and violence, anarchy and cynicism, and it is not an age to try and turn men's eyes to the theories of other men. Even Marx cannot supply a hope that fadeth not away. Mystical evolution or Marxist revolution cannot answer the basic dilemma of man or give a true hope that will make us rejoice and that makes us not ashamed.

The theology of hope to which I want to cling is the same message that is enshrined in Scripture and has cheered the hearts of God's people down the long centuries since He walked the earth with the name of Jesus. Perhaps, to the modern mind, it seems very simple, even naive, but it satisfies my heart, mind and soul. It is a humble faith in God who has revealed Himself in creation, in Scripture and in Christ, His Son. This faith gives me hope — a hope which the world can neither give nor take way. Unashamedly, my hope is in God, in Jesus Christ, His Son, and the Word of God as revealed in Scripture.

Hope in God

'Hope thou in God' was the advice of the psalmist which I have, through God's grace, taken into my heart. My hope is in God, the Maker of heaven and earth, and I know of no greater person or place to put my hope. He is sovereign, Lord of all, and before Him the greatest nations and movements of earth are but 'drops in a bucket' and the inhabitants are like grasshoppers.

He is a God who is working out His purpose and will and can never know defeat, so my hope is one that does not make me ashamed. He is on the throne and rules over all. Perhaps, like faith, it takes a childlike heart to realize the implications — and joy — of such a fact. In China there was a mission school for the children of missionaries which was captured by the Japanese in 1942. The children were then ordered to leave the school and march to an internment camp; as they marched from the playground, carrying cases and their most treasured possessions and toys, they suddenly started to sing. Unprompted by any of the teachers, they marched past the astonished Japanese guards singing lustily:

God is still on the throne, and He will remember His own;
Though trials may press us, and burdens distress us,
He never will leave us alone.
God is still on the throne, and He will remember His own;

His promise is true, He will not forget you,
God is still on the throne.

Those children had a shining faith and burning hope which guns and bayonets could not silence; their hope was in the living, sovereign God. So they could march into a barbed wire internment camp, some never to come out alive, some never to see their parents again on earth, but they could sing in glorious faith and hope of the God who was on the throne and would never leave or forsake them.

No doubt in the eyes of many modern liberal theologians the actions of the children were naive and simple, the result of being indoctrinated with a biblical fundamentalism. It will be considered that the children did not realize the complexities of the faith in the twentieth century and were unaware of the fact that the assured results of modern scholarship had made their simple faith untenable, and their hope unbelievable.

I do not see those children in that light. I see them as standing in a great line of prophets, saints and martyrs who dared to hope in God when, to all intents and purposes, there was no hope. They recall Job who lost everything, yet could still hope in God; David who even in the depths of despair could still hope in God; Shadrach, Meshach and Abednego who asserted that, even if God did not deliver them from the flames of the furnace, they would still hope in God. Considering the pedigree of the children of hope, there is nothing to be ashamed of in daring and living with our hope in God.

My hope is not only in God, but must be in Jesus Christ. Not the Jesus of the liberal theologians who have made him after the image of their own concepts, but in the living Christ, who was alive and was dead and is now alive for evermore. It was He, who after the mockings and scourgings of men, gave His life as a ransom for many. He was the Lamb of God bearing away the sin of the world — and my sin. So my hope is in the Saviour, the Son of God, who loved me and gave Himself for me.

This hope is not in an example, the 'man for others' or the

'living embodiment of love', it is in the Lord of all, because after the resurrection, and before the ascension, Jesus proclaimed that all power, all authority in heaven and on earth was given to Him. He claimed to be Lord and King. The sovereign God has handed over all authority to His Son and He is Lord. Are my hopes not better placed in Him than in all the fine theories and ideas of men?

Then this hope is not for this world, or this life only; if it were so then, as Paul admits, we would be 'of all men most miserable'. There is another world, another life, and even the grim enemy, death, can only mean that the Christian is with Christ 'which is far better'. Not only that, but the kingdom which is already here, in the hearts and lives of the kingdom citizens, will one day be fully established and there will be a new heaven and a new earth. This will come, not through the blood-letting of a revolution, but through the blood of Christ who died to reconcile all things unto Himself.

Compared to all this, the hopes of this world seem trivial and worthless. Even when they are compared with the vague eschatology of liberal theology, the simple Bible-believing hope is infinitely more rational and comforting. It does not rest on complicated concepts and philosophical ideas, that not so much stretch the mind as tend to shatter it with their explosive mixture of sense and non-sense.

My hope is in God and in Christ Jesus and, I must confess, like the psalmist, my hope is in His Word. Certainly I find the Scriptures able to make me wise unto salvation, and profitable for teaching, correction and comfort, but they also give hope. The Word of God is a Word of hope.

So I can read the Scriptures of God and find the ways of God with men. I can see how God acted in human history and how He dealt with His children in days gone by; it is from the same Scriptures that I learn that the God of Abraham, Isaac and Jacob is a living God and changes not, and that Jesus Christ is the same yesterday, today and for ever. In a world of terrorism, national and international, rising crime and violence, I can have hope and find it written by the hand of God. I know I must stand against all injustice

and struggle against those who would devalue and dehumanize man, but my hope is not based on human ideas of
justice or government. My textbook is not the collected
works of Karl Marx or the diaries of Che Guevara but the
written words of God.

My hope is not based on a romantic trust in evolutionary
progress, seeing conflict and pain as necessary stages towards
some bright and glorious future. Equally, I cannot put my
hope in a revolutionary process whereby, in the dialectic of
history and economic forces, all will be well for all manner of
men. Indeed, I must confess that my hope does not rest with
man at all; I know too much about the human heart to lay
my hope there.

Perhaps many will pity my simplicity but I confess that my
hope is in the living God, in His Son, Jesus Christ my Saviour
and Lord and in the Word of God — which cannot be broken.
Without arrogance, I would assert that these statements give
me no cause for shame but can only bring me joy and peace.

Hope is possible in a fallen world, but it must not be
placed there. I have faith, therefore I hope. . .

All you need is love

Dear John,

Thank you for your letter, in which you tell me that you
have moved away from home and made friends with people
who have a 'different moral code' from the one you were
brought up to obey, and you say that you are now expected
to do 'things' which your parents and church taught you
were evil. As this seems to be troubling you, I thought I
should write and give you the benefit of my knowledge,
insight and experience. Let me assure you that you should
not be afraid of fresh experiences or novel ways of expressing
yourself in your new-found maturity. Welcome them! Forget
the stale moral codes of the ancient taboos. Man has now
come of age and there is only one moral code and one ethical
absolute — love. So it doesn't matter what you believe, or
what you say or do, all that matters is love. Base all your life
and actions on the principle of love.

Remember there is nothing unclean, unnatural or evil in
love; all is permissible. Nothing is prohibited in love. Love
can be prostitution, incest, homosexual actions, yes, even
murder, stealing, lying — all things are permitted in love. It
is the ruling principle for God and man. Commit yourself to
love. All you need is love.

Love is a delightful warm glow in the depths of your being.
It is the surge of life in your veins, the intuitional drive of
your heart, the basis of thought and the very ground of your
being. Love is tenderness and demanding, giving and taking,

115

caring and being careless. Yes, my boy, love is all things and love is everything human.

So with love go out and enjoy and conquer life. Laugh at parents, church and society who have tried to burden you with an endless list of 'Do's and Don't's. Be a man and dare to love. Perhaps we can talk about this soon. With remission of time for good conduct I should be out of here soon. It is tragic that the law courts of our land are still so unenlightened that they do not recognize love as a valid defence for all things,

Yours in love

Your affectionate Uncle Theo.

8
Love—I believe in love

Hope may not be a word on many lips today, but the word 'love' is used almost endlessly in every stratum of society. Pop singers howl, weep and rage about it; poets declaim it; psychologists analyse it, and even philosophers pontificate on its meaning and purpose. Theologians are no exception. They may extol the virtues of doubt and the complications of hope, but they are strong on the teaching of love. Many of their contributions to theology seem to begin and end with love.

I accept this emphasis on love; only a fool would dare to suggest that love has no place in the Christian life and, whatever may be thought to the contrary, I am no fool. So when anyone, liberal or Bible-believing, speaks and writes about love, I am sympathetic and understanding. In a world of hate and bitterness, disrespect and arrogance, I recognize a desperate shortage of real, simple, old-fashioned love.

Yet here again, as in so many areas of liberal doctrine and theology, I find suspicion arising in my heart and an intellectual unease invading my mind. There can be no doubt that the teaching of the modern theologians is somewhat confusing compared to the plain and simple outlook which I find sufficient for daily living in seeking to be a faithful servant of the Lord. The basic trouble is that I am never quite sure what exactly they are talking about; of course, this may be a poor reflection on my mental capability, but I doubt if this can be the full explanation. Love should not be a complicated concept.

Although it sounds like a pop song, I believe 'Love is the

greatest thing,' so why should I feel unhappy about the attitude of liberal theologians to love? They have done one of two things with it. Either they have loaded the word with so much new content that it is incapable of bearing such a burden, or they have removed all content from it so that it simply ceases to have any meaning or validity. They have either deified love or reduced it to a mere philosophical concept.

Is love God?

I suspect that they have almost deified love. It has become the only absolute for all understanding and activity. The Shorter Catechism may have seen man's chief end as being to glorify God and enjoy Him for ever, but that is probably too biblically orientated and simplistically old-fashioned for many modern scholars. They would argue that man's chief end is to love, and love is the purpose, reason and meaning of life. If you love, then nothing else matters. It does not matter what you do, say, think or even what you believe — as long as you love. So love is the ground of our being, the basis of all life and the affinity of being with being.

They therefore tell me that the only crime is not to love. I must confess that such a statement does make my eyebrows rise and troublesome questions throb in my mind. Under the Nazi regime something like six million Jews were murdered; in terms of some liberal theology can it be true that Hitler's only crime was that he lacked love? The young man reported in this morning's newspaper, who attacked a young girl, raped her and left her half dead; should I not see him as vile and evil, but simply as a young man who lacks love? Should there be no law against murder, assault, theft, rape, or even no speed limits, but only one all-embracing law forbidding 'not to love'?

Perhaps this 'theology of love' is very profound and can lead to interesting discussion and endless debate, but it is too complicated — or too simple — for my mind. I do not believe that love is the only virtue and I certainly do not believe that not to love is the only crime.

What disturbs me about this emphasis on love is that the implication is that we should not obey God, but love. Love becomes God. Love becomes the standard and measurement of all things. To talk about 'obeying the impulse to love' and to be 'open to love' sounds good orthodox Christianity as well as ethically sound, but I am left wondering if there is not the grave danger that the Lord God Almighty, Maker of heaven and earth, is left out in the cold. Rather than a love that finds its source in the God of love, and that is directed towards Him and His love reflected from our hearts to the world, it becomes man-centred. I suspect it becomes almost an idol.

Recently I heard a minister making an impassioned plea for love and service in the community. He was engaged in a team ministry in a socially deprived area, one of the new blights on the landscape — huge soulless housing estates where people are herded together without community or fellowship. The human problems and the social needs were great and as he appealed for a vision of what could be done my heart warmed towards him. We live in an age where there is no vision and the people are perishing. But as the minister began to develop his vision and make his call for service in love, I did not feel challenged or inspired. Truth to tell, I became depressed and sad.

There was no God in his vision. It was all love and service purely on a horizontal plane. His vision was of the church being immersed in the political and social problems of our age, turning away from self to serve others in love. 'Serving others in love' was, he asserted, what Christianity is all about. This is certainly a simplistic assertion which I cannot accept.

As I am intensely conscious of how easy it is for words to be misunderstood, I should make it clear I am in full agreement with the call for Christian involvement in the social, political, economic and cultural facets of our society. I agree wholeheartedly with the call to serve in love. But a one-dimensional love cannot do it, and this is the root of the fallacy.

As I read and hear the many noble words on love coming at me from so many directions I find that, instead of my eyes being opened, my mind becomes clouded. We seem to be using the same words but speaking different languages. While I find it hard to disagree with so much that is said, there is the uncomfortable sensation of alarm bells ringing deep in my sub-conscious mind and my rationality hovers on the brink of absurdity. A simple and yet tortuous question bores its way into my mind: what is love? Everything? Nothing?

I suspect that the modern liberal theologians, by almost deifying love, treating it as the only absolute for all and everything, have indulged in something approaching linguistic vandalism. They have added so much graffiti to the beautiful word 'love' that it has become almost ugly and without shape or form. So the simple, and easily understood concept of love has been encrusted with mystical or intellectually baffling language. They tell me that the ultimate and only criterion for human conduct is not a moral code, but a selfless and sacrificial *agape* love; that all assertions about God are, in the last analysis, assertions about love, and the ground and meaning of all personal relationships is love. So there should be no prescriptive laws, no prohibitions or commandments, only love meeting every situation on its own merits.

But graffiti, even intellectual graffiti, are still a form of vandalism. It seems to me that the tender word 'love' has been burdened with so much content that it has collapsed under the weight, expiring as a valid concept for our age. The problem is that if love covers and means everything human then it ends by meaning nothing in particular. It becomes an empty vessel, waiting to be filled with our own ideas and desires: a word without content, reflecting whatever meaning we wish to impose upon it.

Although all this may be taken as a sign of ignorance, or even of anti-intellectualism, I must assert that I do not suffer from a phobia which makes me fear 'big' words. I accept the obvious fact that technical books cannot be written without technical language; philosophy cannot be taught without the use of philosophical concepts and theology must use theological terminology. But, simplistic as it may seem, I believe that words should be used to clarify and reveal, not to confuse and conceal. So I suspect that the rich robes heaped upon the 'King Love' of modern thought are like the emperor's new robes of the fairy tale and I am tempted to act the part of the little boy and scream with laughter.

Yet the screams of laughter are mingled with screams of terror. I do not want to drown in the depths of philosophy or be blinded by the smoke-screen of words. I want reality. I want a simple answer to a simple question: what is love?

And the greatest of these

If, in accordance with modern theories, all laws and commandments should be ignored and love taken as the only authority, then what guidance is there as to how we should love? Is each person capable of making his own interpretation? This would require a great faith in the innate ability of men to do the right thing at the right time — and at every opportunity. I confess a lack of faith in that direction. It seems to me that love must have guidance and limitations or it degenerates into lust and self-indulgence. How then do we know love and how to act in love?

Again the modern liberal theologians use the same words as myself and yet speak a different language; they are not silenced by my questing after the norms of love. They point to Jesus, who they tell me, was the man of love, the man for others, the man who showed the ethic of love in all things. As in so much else of their teaching I find myself being pulled in opposite directions by the same argument.

The teachers who tell me to follow the ethical Jesus, to be a man of love as He was a man of love, are the same people who have already told me that I cannot accept the stories of Jesus as either authoritative or trustworthy. The events recorded in the Gospels and the teaching of Jesus are not to be taken as factual, but seen as the group theology of the early church or the imaginative recreations of first-century man. So I am presented with two Messiahs.

There is the Jesus who taught and practised love. He welcomed outcasts and children, cared for people, spoke words of love and compassion. This is the real Jesus for the liberal theologian, the man of love for the liberal theology. The Jesus who did miracles, spoke of hell-fire and coming judgement, died and rose again — this not the real Jesus of liberalism, but the creation of first-century theologians who were not as wise or clever as their counterparts in the twentieth century.

Again such an exegetical methodology must be questioned. For a long time now, those of liberal theological persuasion have condemned evangelicals for depending upon 'proof texts', accusing them, sometimes justly, of taking individual texts out of context to prove some particular point of doctrine. I find it more than ironic that liberals are now practising the same technique. In praise of love they are taking texts and incidents from the life of Jesus and from the Bible generally, and are using them, without reference to context, to bolster up their own theories and viewpoints. So they pick certain events and actions in the life of Jesus and say, 'This is how love should act,' and other incidents, which do not fit into the theory, are discarded as being later additions by a theologically ignorant editor of the first or second century.

But while I believe Jesus was a man of love, I also believe He was a man of justice and judgement and there is no contradiction or problem in such an understanding. The whipping of the moneychangers from the temple was as much an act of love as giving sight to the blind or making a lame man walk. His warnings of judgement and hell were just as much words of love as His promises of peace and rest. The Jesus of the Gospels was a consistent character because, at least to me, love must include condemnation, judgement and even punishment. Even at a human level chastisement, in some form or another, is a necessary part of parental love.

In the final analysis this pointing to Jesus as an example of love fails to recognize His mission and purpose. If He came purely as an example then we must be, of all men, most miserable. It means that we depend upon our own strength as we struggle to love and be good; not only must we interpret the way as best we can, but by ourselves must create a pattern of behaviour by our understanding of a man who lived and died long, long ago. Then, to complicate this even further, those who hold this view tell us that we cannot treat as completely trustworthy the records of this man's life and death — the man we are to follow! Not only that, but we must then approach each situation as if it was a 'thing in itself' and apply the 'logic of love' which we have learned from the 'man of love' as revealed in testimony of doubtful witnesses in the Gospels. It is not God and the law which should govern all our actions — it is love and the situation.

No doubt this sounds clever and modern but I rather suspect that it is such theories which have led to the confusion in the spheres of morality and ethics today. The simple way of love has become complicated and almost incomprehensible. Indeed, this new morality of love is not a shining pathway, but a trackless desert.

Perhaps it is true that the 'new morality' where love was the only absolute is no longer as popular as it was, but it has left behind much that has muddied the waters and obscured the guiding stars. All morality and personal behaviour, which we were then told had to be governed by love alone, have now become matters of debate and discussion. Increasingly God and His Word can be left out of the debate and matters can be decided by majority vote. It is assumed that love will always know how to act, although the way love is defined means that one can act anyway one pleases or can be justified according to the situation. Or, and this is equally dangerous, it is defined as such a complicated philosophical proposition that it is beyond the wit of ordinary mortals either to appreciate or understand it.

But, without apologies for my simplicity, I do not believe that love is such a difficult concept to understand. Even the youngest of children know something of love and can appreciate the actions of love; they know when they are loved and are capable of loving. It is not a childish emotion but something all men and women are capable of doing. But it must be said that, simplistic though I may be, I am too much a child of the twentieth century not to be aware of the challenge facing Christians today. There are agonizing choices to be made and often there seems to be no easy answer, but the path of love is not the way of our own understanding; it is the way of obedience.

Jesus said, 'If you love me then keep my commandments,' and love acts according to the laws and norms laid down by God. In the final analysis we are to love one another, not because it is the best thing to do, the natural thing to do, or even because it is the thing we want to do — we are to love because we are commanded to love. And God never commands us to do anything He will not give strength and grace to carry out. So if we love God and believe His Word — and to love someone surely means you believe what they say — then we have a map and signposts and the Holy Spirit of God to be our guide and light to our path. By His grace He will give us power even to love our enemies.

But our love must be centred upon God and this is what is lacking in the modern understanding of love and acting in love. It is all man-centred and the text that is thrown at me, 'Love your neighbour as yourself,' is a 'proof text' out of context with a vengeance! In fact it is one of the oldest tricks in the unfair debater's handbook — quoting half a statement and giving the impression that it is the whole proposition.

Thou shalt love

The actual words of our Lord, summing up the whole law of God, were, '. . . Thou shalt love the Lord thy God with all thy heart, and with all thy soul, and with all thy mind, and with all thy strength, this is the first commandment, and the second is like, namely this, Thou shalt love thy neighbour as thyself.'

Yet it is a sad fact that on almost every hand today I am told to obey the second commandment while the first one is passed over in silence. The first, the prime commandment is ignored and so many modern Christian teachers are saying things which no self-respecting humanist would deny. But the Christian faith is not man-centred and Christian love is not man-centred — Jesus said we should first love God and then our neighbour.

I am aware that many who are clever in modern theology will accuse me of playing with words because I have been assured that I can only love God through my neighbour. But if this is so then it is Jesus who must have been mistaken; he made love to God and love to neighbours into separate commandments. It may be He was speaking cryptically so that it takes a course in contemporary theology to understand the meaning of His words, but I am content to take the words at their plain value and meaning. He did not say that we were to love our neighbour and, through him, love God.

God must come first and this seems to be the whole biblical emphasis in all things — our faith, worship, service, actions and love must all take place in a God-centred context. The commandments given to Moses placed God first, the prophets placed God before all things, religious, social and political, and Jesus placed love to God as the prime commandment. It is God who must have the pre-eminence in all things — not man or his neighbour.

As I understand it, the whole Christian life must be lived on the basic assumption that it is God who comes first in all our human life. We start with the fact of God, triune, infinite and personal, our relationship to Him, our duty and responsibility to Him and His Word, and from that should spring all our actions and thoughts. Even love is not exempt. So this love is more than a warm affection or an emotional experience, though it includes that if we are to take the words of Jesus seriously. He has commanded us to love God with our heart, soul, mind and strength; as total beings we have to love God totally.

We are commanded to love God with all our heart. Now I know that traditionally the heart has been seen as the seat of affections and emotions and is still a common way of expressing our deepest feelings. If it were not so then most of our pop song writers and lyricists would be out of business.

But in the Bible the heart is seen as much more than the source of love and human emotions; it is the root and ground-base of the human personality. It is from the heart that all faith and action come and, as Jesus reminded us, from the heart of man spring the issues of life and both good and evil. So when we are commanded to love God with all our heart it means that the root and ground of our being is to be rooted and grounded in God. Love towards God is to be the mainspring of all our thoughts and actions.

Of course, this does not exclude the emotions; yet if I talk of loving God in a heart-warming way I am liable to be accused of being emotionally irrational. But the two disciples on the road to Emmaus on the first Easter found that their hearts were strangely warmed as they walked and talked with the risen Christ. At the same time, Peter's confession, 'Lord, you know I love you,' must have been an emotional expression of his heart. So it seems to me that it cannot be wrong to respond in an emotional way to the love of God and to love Him with the feelings and emotions which He has given us. I find it a strange paradox that, in our bewildering century, we endlessly sing of emotions, use them to sell through advertising, to manipulate and dehumanize, and yet are suspicious of emotion in religion. But it is a command-ment: we are to love God with our hearts.

Then we are commanded to love God with all our souls. In the closed universe of the twentieth century, where one-dimensional man lives a lonely life in the masses of the global village, it seems folly even to talk about the soul. A spiritual dimension to life is avoided in most modern thought and even, it seems, in some modern theology. Or, rather than completely avoided, it is treated as totally mystical beyond the realms of rational thought. But man is not an animal or a piece of self-conscious vegetation; in the beginning God breathed into man and he became a 'living soul'. There is a spiritual side to the human personality and our love to God must have this spiritual dimension. We are to love God with our souls, responding to God who is a Spirit.

So our love is not bound by the physical universe, just as

our faith is not limited to the material world. There is a valid 'other-worldliness' to which we should respond and confess: loving God with our souls, knowing that all of eternity lies before us to express and explore that love.

We are also to love God with all our minds. No one can doubt that the intellectual capacity of man is great; the evidence is all around in the world which man has made. He is great, his mind can encompass the universe and, even in a fallen world, man has great potential and possibilities. So it is no surprise to read the words of our Lord that man should love God with his mind.

As I understand it, this means that our intellectual processes are to be submitted to the Spirit of God, seeking as an expression of our love to obey Him in all things. After all, the fear of the Lord is the beginning of wisdom and this fear, or awe, means that we will love, respect and obey His Word even in the very thought that we entertain in our minds. Paul advised us to seek to make every thought captive to Christ and that would appear to be a real submission of love.

Then we are to love God with all our strength, and I would take this to mean our bodies as well as our mental or spiritual strength. God not only made us 'living souls', but shaped and fashioned us as physical bodies. Certainly the Bible knows nothing of the Platonic division which sets up a dichotomy between the physical and spiritual, with the spiritual being higher and better. Our bodies and the physical creation were all made by God and seen by Him to be 'very good'. Although sin has corrupted all things, the whole creation now groaning and our bodies subject to decay and death, yet the redemption in Christ will bring salvation to the fallen world and new and perfect bodies to all God's children.

Meanwhile we, who know Christ as Saviour and Lord, can love God with our bodies; all our physical abilities and capabilities can be used as an expression of love and service to Him. Our physical strength and natural talents can and should be used to His glory; indeed Paul has told us that the mundane, physical necessary things such as eating and drinking can be done to the glory of God and, as such, surely are an expression of our love. We are to love God with all our strength.

It seems to me that there is a perfect balance here. Heart, soul, mind and body make the complete man who was made and commanded to love God completely. The secularist, who would reduce everything to the body, and the pietist, who would make everything spiritual, are both condemned; so is the liberal who would make man into a social animal who can only love through his fellow animals. We are to love God as full and complete men — hearts, souls, minds and bodies. Every aspect of the human personality was made for God and intended to respond in love towards Him.

With the prime commandment fulfilled, then the secondary one follows almost automatically. If we truly love God, whom we have not seen, then we must love our brothers and neighbours whom we can see; this must be true because a right relationship with God must logically mean a correct relationship with all His creatures.

But I must confess a suspicion that in much modern theology, as in modern humanism, the ignoring of the prime commandment and the emphasis on the secondary one seem like the age-old attempt to keep God comfortably far away. As in all else, without God, love ceases to have meaning and when it is seen as man-centred then it is liable to be destructive and a curse rather than a blessing and freedom. For love is not an emotion, it is a way of life; it is not a theory but a practice; it is not a concept, but a response to Almighty God and His Son who loved us and gave Himself for us.

There are faith, hope and love, and the greatest of these. . .

Nightmare
New law for the new age

Then the word of the electronic computer came
unto me saying,
'Hear the word which I declare unto you, the word
of the law which you have conceived in your own
heart and is the desire of all men.
Thou shalt have no gods before thee, and shalt live
as if thou wert a god.
Thou shalt make great and glorious images and
shalt worship the works of thy hands, the achievements of thy genius and the glory of thine own
name.
Thou shalt not worry about taking the name of the
Lord thy God in vain; is it not better upon thy lips
than in thy mind?
Remember the sabbath day and enjoy thyself
therein. Five days shalt thou labour and do all thy
work and on the sixth day thou shalt worship the
great god sport and shout thy hosannas to those
who play before thee. But on the sabbath day thou
shalt lie long in bed and seek recreation in the
place of thy heart's desire.
Thou shalt forget thy father and thy mother and
seek thy own generation, for the young must not
be tied to the old.
Thou shalt not fear to commit murder for political
ends, for the action of freedom fighters can always
be justified.

Thou shalt not fear to commit adultery, for what profit is in chastity or fidelity? So be not afraid to take her who is not thy wife lest thou find thyself impoverished by the Freudian sins of repression and fixations.

Thou shalt not steal anything of great value, but thou mayest take thy employer's time, thy employer's stationery, and thy employer's goods. And thou mayest take into thy possession whatsoever thou findest on the highway or wherever no one is looking.

Thou shalt not fear to bear false witness, for what interest is to be found in truth? Are not the tongues of gossip more to be desired than the painful words of truth?

Thou shalt covet thy neighbour's house, thy neighbour's furnishings and all thy neighbour's goods. Are not progress and economic development dependent upon thy coveting what thou lackest? Thus shalt thou have full employment and earn the praise of the advertisers.'

Then as I heard the voice of the electronic computer speak these words, behold there came a flash of fire as from heaven and then it was dark and great was the darkness thereof. And it came to pass in the darkness a voice came unto me saying, 'Lo, a fuse has blown!'

9
Sin—And I believe there is a devil

It is a fact, doubtless much to the dismay of many modern scholars, that the Bible persists in treating sin and iniquity as if they were positive forces at work in the world and in the hearts of men. Perhaps even more disturbing to these men, the Bible frequently records the activity of the devil and demons, treating them as real spiritual creatures in active rebellion against God and all His works in creation. As with so much else in modern liberal theology, it is taken as self-evident that modern theories cannot be wrong, so the biblical evidence must be treated as revealing a primitive understanding of reality which is completely unacceptable to the truly contemporary mind.

On the principle that what cannot be explained should be explained away, many Christian teachers of our day have spent a great deal of time and effort trying to abolish the devil from Christian thought and to discard the orthodox doctrine of sin from the Christian creed. While they may have presented many interesting theories and imaginative, though conflicting, ideas, two things seem to unite them all: there is no personal devil, and sin, whatever it may be, is not sin. So what the Bible makes plain is now treated as if it was not plain at all, and what the church has accepted for centuries is now treated as not being worthy of serious thought.

What happened to the devil?

I have therefore been told that it must not be thought that there is actually such a person as the devil, and that it is only the simple untutored mind which would take such a primitive biblical concept as factual. I have been assured, on the basis of the finest modern scholarship, that Satan, the devil, is just a symbolic figure, a personalized myth to explain the presence of so much evil and suffering in the world.

The tempter in the garden and the tempter in the wilderness at the beginning of the Old and New Testaments, are not to be understood as real creatures, but characters in a parabolic story to illustrate existential truth. Equally when Peter spoke about the devil going about the world·like a roaring lion or disguised as an angel of light, he was just using figurative language, creating a verbal image to emphasize a point. The fact that Peter did not think he was using figurative language does not matter — that is how we are supposed to take it today.

Admittedly, when we read the Gospels, it seems obvious that Jesus believed in a literal devil, but this is no great problem to those followers today who find it incredible that God should communicate to us through an infallible Word. So they have told me that Jesus used figurative speech, even though it obviously misled His disciples into believing that He was speaking factually. Alternatively, there is the theory that, because Jesus was a first-century figure who did not have the benefit of modern scientific knowledge or an understanding of parapsychology, it is not surprising that he accepted such primitive ideas as personal demons and a devil. Then, of course, they fall back on the liberal final line of defence: Jesus said nothing about the devil; anything attributed to Him on that subject must have been added later by redactors who thought they knew what He should have said on every possible topic.

No doubt each of these theories has its attraction for some, but I prefer the simple and plain solution and willingly accept that Jesus believed there was an adversary, Satan, the devil, who was the enemy of God and man. This belief has been carried down the centuries. Certainly, historically, the people of God have always believed there was a personal being of evil, ever seeking to destroy and deceive, and that he had at his command legions of demons to carry out his work. Scholars accepted the reality of the devil and knew they could only face him in the strong name of Jesus.

But now, it seems, those days have gone. We must not believe that the devil is a real person and the words of the Bible and the faith of the church for centuries must not be taken as true. The devil has gone. Perhaps it has been a slow process, but it appears that in our age man has finally got rid of the devil who has haunted and degraded men ever since the Fall.

At least one of the biographers of the Scots poet, Robert Burns, has suggested that one of his greatest achievements was to laugh the devil out of hell and banish him from Scots Presbyterian theology. Knowing something of contemporary Scots theology I must confess this seems to be true — the devil has been banished. Indeed he has been banished from almost all modern liberal theology. Yet I must assert that it seems to be grossly unfair to give all the credit to Burns; many theologians, without the gift of wit and satire which Burns showed, have happily helped in the process of getting rid of the devil. They did not laugh him out of existence but coldly explained him away. Since they started with the assumption that he could not possibly exist, it was not hard to accumulate arguments and reasons to prove that the devil had not only departed but had never been; so he was gone, unmourned and unwept.

Without apologies for the simplicity of the question I find myself facing a serious problem to which I have found no answer. If indeed the devil has gone — then who is carrying on the business? No one can doubt that the business of evil and sin is continuing and even prospering. I find it hard to believe that I live in a world where there is no devil.

I am a child of the twentieth century. I have lived through the Spanish Civil War, the Italian invasion of Ethiopia, the Japanese war in China, the Second World War, Korea, Burma, Biafra, Vietnam, Northern Ireland and all the other 'bush wars' with which our planet is plagued. Herod may have killed his dozens at Bethlehem but our abortion clinics can kill their thousands daily; Nero may have killed his thousands, but today we can kill in millions. They say there is no devil and yet I have lived in the age of Buchenwald, Belsen and Dachau; the age of Hitler, Stalin, Mussolini and Amin; a time when crime takes on the face of innocence under the guise of some great cause or humanitarian movement.

Not only have I seen the growth of war, international crime and terrorism, and apparently endless acts of savage destruction upon completely innocent people, but in my own land I see the now almost steady growth of lawlessness. Crimes against property and people increase, and sexual assaults and vandalism sweep the nation like new plagues. When groups disagree, they no longer consider their opponents merely to be mistaken or misled, but see them as evil and malevolent, objects of hate.

All this is taking place all around me; there is no way I can escape noticing it, yet seeing this evidence, I am expected to believe there is no devil. I am expected to come to the conclusion that the orthodox teaching of the Bible and the church, that there are spiritual powers and beings working towards the triumph of evil, is all wrong. Is it really just a debating point to ask who, if the devil is gone, is carrying on his work?

Tragically, I must confess, the evidence is not all outside my own heart and life. I have known the force and power of the Evil One in my own heart and mind and in the midst of temptation it is no help to study the philosophical and theological reasons for not believing in the devil. I know him, not as an academic concept revealed in Scripture alone, but in my existential experience of life in a fallen world.

There is a devil at loose in the world, and he cannot be abolished by majority academic vote or banished by any new theology. He was the tempter from the beginning and is still tempting men — even to the extent of making them doubt his existence. After all, would this not be the perfect strategy for the Evil One — to pretend he does not exist and is merely an old-fashioned myth?

So in spite of all the evidence to the contrary, the devil has no place in modern liberal theology or in twentieth-century thought. But it is much more than the devil that has gone. Sin itself has been explained away in a myriad of theories. Where it is not totally denied it has been killed off by the 'death of a thousand qualifications'.

Is sin just not good?

In an age which will not let God be God or truth be true, it is not surprising that sin is not considered to be sin. Rather than lawlessness, a refusal to obey God, sin is seen today as purely unsocial acts which are the result of social deprivation; a form of social maladjustment, mental aberration or merely a genetic problem. Many, in our age, are like the character in Wilde's play who was brought up to call a spade an 'agricultural implement', so sin has become estrangement from being, or part of becoming — a nice intellectual phrase to embrace the evolutionary idea of developing from the old beast. Sin has become psychological, not moral; environmental, not part of man; social, not personal, or it is a psychological philosophical concept, not a fact. Or even, most incredible of all, it is presented as the absence of good.

So I have been assured that sin must be seen as being essentially a negative and not a positive force. Sin is just the absence of good. I must confess I find this a mind-blowing proposition. Logically it means that I should not consider Hitler an evil man — he was just not good. Then if sin is the absence of good it seems reasonable to suppose that pain must be the absence of joy; tears the absence of laughter; rain the absence of sunshine, and rape to be merely the absence of love. If it is seriously held that sin is the absence of good then I know no good reason why the proposition should not be reversed and why it should not be argued that goodness is the absence of evil.

But I find it hard to comprehend how anyone, living in our century, can hold to the strange dogma that sin is not a positive force, both destructive and powerful, corrupting individuals as well as nations, and bringing pain and havoc into the lives of millions. It seems to me self-evident that sin exists in the world, and the universality of guilt feelings in mankind throughout the whole world does prove something.

I rather suspect that most modern examinations of the problem of sin, by theologians as well as psychologists, have concentrated on seeking an explanation of guilt feelings without admitting the possibility of the reality of guilt. The challenge has been to explain sin and guilt without any reference to God. It has all been reduced to a matter of anthropology or some other science which gives scope for wonderful and weird theories. So the guilt that lies in the heart of man and the dark sins which lie deep, tempting and fascinating, are seen as the taboos of the 'primal horde' and the echoes of a primitive past. All these can only offer an explanation, not a solution; they, like the best medical quacks, can treat the symptoms while the disease rages unabated.

The basic problem of the existence of sin and evil in the world is not to explain it, but to find a cure. If we see it as metaphysical rather than moral, a necessary limitation of being finite creatures, then there is no cure. It is all part of the glory and horror of being human.

The logical end of all this, of course, is the denial of any personal responsibility. Yet are we not devaluing men and women by seeing them as automatons who are not responsible for their actions? Indeed the whole modern theory of punishment today, aided and supported by many theologians, is based upon the necessity of treatment, not punishment, for sinful action. The criminal is never really wholly to blame for his behaviour; it was his genes, his environment or his social conditioning which made him act the way he did. Owing to the pressures to which he was subject, he could not really help robbing the bank, hitting the cashier with a pickaxe and knocking down an old woman as he ran away. So when he is caught it is more important that he be treated as a sick man than as a morally responsible creature who is answerable for his actions. Treatment for social ills, not punishment for evil acts, dominates so much thinking today about sin. Yet if this approach is valid and true then a double standard is in operation. Medals, awards and admiration are given to those who do good and brave deeds; yet it must be presumed that they were just acting according to their genes, environment and social conditioning in exactly the same way as the sick criminal.

But more important than what modern theories of sin are doing to individuals and the social community is their effect on the gospel of Jesus Christ. If there is no sin, in the sense of moral rebellion against God, then the gospel has no good news for mankind and the cross of Christ has no effect. It means that Jesus Christ was not the Lamb of God bearing away the sin of the world and He was not made sin for us. The preaching of the cross does, indeed, become complete foolishness and the gospel is denied.

Indeed much of the Bible then becomes meaningless and many events can be little more than foolishness. Many have been inspired by the great prayer of Stephen for his murderers: 'Lord, lay not this sin to their charge.' What on earth — or in heaven — can these words mean if those who were throwing the stones were simply being estranged from the ground of their being? Is it not meaningless if they were psychologically and socially conditioned to act that way? Rather than a great and noble prayer, it becomes a silly cry to ask forgiveness for men who were acting in a way they could not help but act. But if sin is a positive reality, if it is a deliberate choice, then the prayer of Stephen becomes a glorious expression of love and faith, showing a man willing to pray for those who sinned against God and himself.

According to the Bible, in the final analysis, all sin is against God, an act of rebellion against the Sovereign Lord of all. David recognized this; after committing adultery and arranging the death of Uriah, David repented and prayed, 'Against thee, thee only have I sinned.' Certainly the Bible shows that sin may have social and personal effects and implications, but sin is basically transgression against the laws of God; it is man seeking to be autonomous, to go his own way, do his own thing and be as a god himself.

All men are sinners; this is the clear teaching of the Word of God. In the beginning Adam and Eve wanted to 'be as God' and through them sin has infected every heart and permeated the world. Again this will show something of my simplicity — I believe in original sin. Such a conviction, while it may be denied by many modern theologians, seems to me to be true to the Scriptures and the reality of the world in which I live. Certainly it is true of my own heart.

As the little girl asked, 'Mummy, why is there something in me that always wants to be naughty?' I can appreciate something of what the girl meant, knowing it of my own experience. That thing the Bible calls 'sin', and all attempts to make it something else are a vain effort to evade the reality and can only make the condition worse. In spite of all the clever words of clever men it is plain, old-fashioned, biblical sin which is at the root of the human dilemma, the alienation and helplessness of man — even in the twentieth century.

So I believe that all have sinned and have come far short of the glory God intended for them. But this cannot be the final word for man because I know from the same Scriptures, which reveal the reality of sin, that there is grace and forgiveness. In the words of the Creed, 'I believe in the forgiveness of sin' and this means much more than psychological relief from guilt feelings. How can I ask for forgiveness for a metaphysical concept, a psychological condition, finite limitation or alienation? I believe in sin and guilt, the universality of these things and, simple though it may seem, believe that men feel guilty because they are guilty!

Freedom from the chains of sin

In the eighteenth century Rousseau saw men born free and yet everywhere in chains; he blamed the political and social systems for man's slavery. I suspect his condemnation has now been taken up by the new theological Marxists or Marxist theologians who, going much further than Augustine's 'just war', are embracing a 'just terrorism'.

Freedom from sin is now promised through revolution and new political structures.

As I am not completely out of touch with the reality of the world in which I live, I accept that there are chains of political exploitation. All men are to some extent victims of their social conditioning, but this is not the root cause of the human predicament. Men indeed are slaves, not to systems or forms of government, but to sin. It is sin which holds men captive. The inborn desire to live our own lives, actively and deliberately refusing to obey God or His Word, is the real captive condition of mankind.

This will not be changed by substituting a new environment or by violently overthrowing any political system. The tragic truth is that any system established by sinful men must end up by being a sinful system. Then, of course, all this is ignoring the facts that freedom is promised and available in Christ alone. So while it may be necessary for Christians to struggle for political and social justice, it is naive to imagine that these things can ever bring true liberty and freedom.

Equally it is foolish to think that by redefining words then freedom can be assured; yet such is the folly of our age that many are engaged in such a task. Ironically this idiotic behaviour was foretold by the secular prophet, George Orwell, who in his nightmare *1984* showed a world where, through the new language of 'Newspeak', it was assumed that if you called a thing by a different name it became something quite different. Although there are a few years to go before we reach 1984 this is already happening.

The medieval church formulated a list of seven deadly sins which have now been reinterpreted to suit the morality of the new age. The seven sins were pride, covetousness, envy, wrath, gluttony, sloth and lechery. These can now be happily incorporated into the acceptable social, and even Christian standards. Pride is to be understood as a healthy self-respect; covetousness has become justifiable ambition and legitimate aspirations; envy has been raised to a political right; wrath is really moral and righteous indignation; gluttony becomes merely a healthy appetite for the consumer society; sloth is necessary relaxation, and lechery is accepted as sophistication and broadmindedness in the permissive age.

Perhaps it it not surprising that I find myself in an age where there is moral confusion and spiritual anarchy. Words have not only been devalued, but twisted and corrupted so much that they no longer seem to mean what they say. If we call sin by another name the fact is that it still remains sin; the language of our hearts and consciences condemns us and the language of Scripture is clear and plain.

Probably the greatest attempt to evade sin by redefining it has come from the school of 'situation ethics'. Commandments and laws disappear and true freedom is reached as each person is allowed to act, in love, according to the situation. All that matters is love and the only criterion is the actual situation.

As I have been accused of being a 'hard-liner' in matters of morality I should confess an awareness of a truly biblical situational ethic which is Christian and valid. But this is always still within boundaries and limitations. There are clearly defined parameters and there are still absolutes. But to assert, as these new ethical teachers tell us, that anything and everything can be permitted is to move far on the road to disaster and self-interest.

Only an age which has almost deified sex could find Christian teachers saying that adultery, in certain situations, is perfectly permissible. If anything is permissible then in what circumstances could a sexual assault on a child be justified? Love is the only absolute — so what if there was love both in child and adult? I will not continue this line of argument, knowing that my critics will rejoice to see how, like all Bible believers, I have equated sin with sex and have revealed my true colours as a Puritan prude or a Victorian hypocrite. But the questions raised by the theory of situation ethics are wider than sexual behaviour. Certainly the questions that arise in my mind are many and varied.

In the Bible we are told to care for the stranger within the gates, to provide for the fatherless and the widows, to deny ourselves, not to be slothful in business, not to avenge ourselves, not to conform to this world and to worship the Lord our God and Him alone. Now in terms of situation ethics, where love is the only absolute, it is possible that there are times when we would be perfectly justified in not caring for the strangers and immigrants within our land. Should we be content to let the fatherless and the widows starve, be slothful in business, get our own back by acts of vengeance, conform to the standards and thought patterns of the world and perhaps even worship other gods? I confess my imagination cannot conceive such a situation arising where we can break these laws and still claim to be justified.

Freedom is not to be found by getting rid of all absolutes or by smashing down the old barriers. Doing that makes the Christian ethic become an irrational adventure where all laws can be transgressed and all commandments broken. The result is not liberty but chaos, anarchy and sin abounding.

In view of all this, perhaps it will be appreciated why I want to hold to the simple, even if it is old-fashioned, view of sin. I want to hold to the biblical view, not the new theories produced by sinful men to hide the fact of sin. The Bible does not glamourize sin, but recognizes it as a cancer which is totally destructive and positively deadly.

Nor does the Bible treat me as a poor helpless victim of some psychological disorder which is beyond my will. Rather it treats me with a great deal of respect, seeing me as a morally responsible being, fully conscious and aware of my actions. Yet the Bible recognizes that I am a sinner, a slave of sin, and through the grace of God it offers pardon and freedom. Only in Christ is there true freedom. Through His death I can know the forgiveness of God, the cleansing and strength to walk in the paths of righteousness for His name's sake.

So those clever in the modern understanding of the faith may tell me that there is no devil and that sin is not really sin, but I will simply hold to the words of Scripture. The Word of God leaves me with no illusions: the devil is mighty and sin is powerful and positive in the world and in my heart. But, through His grace, the people of God are called to wrestle against the powers of evil in high places. They are not called to rewrite the Word of God or pretend that it does not mean what it says. Sin is sin and there can be forgiveness and freedom.

I know there are many who find it hard to believe the plain words of Scripture. It seems more intellectual to treat it as a cryptic crossword full of mysterious symbols and philosophical clues and so they take the devil to be a personified myth and sin to be an expression of the limitation of finitehood, estrangement from being or just the negation of good. Yet other words condemn such a view — the words of our daily newspapers. Daily the headlines proclaim that someone is carrying on the work of the devil and all the news items reveal the facts and effects of sin. It may well be that my daily newspaper is simply reflecting myths, legends and primitive ideas, but I must confess a complete inability to accept such a thesis.

So I believe in the reality of sin and the existence of the devil; even in the twentieth century, perhaps even especially in the twentieth century, I see no need to apologize for such a simple biblical belief.

Ichabod—the glory has departed

Memo: from the Contemporary Consultative Council.

Subject: The state of the church.

The following are brief observations and suggestions on the best way to make the twentieth-century church effective and, in the words of our remit, 'trendy and with-it'.

Preliminary observations

1.   The primary need is a new image. The church is largely irrelevant because it is burdened with out-of-date doctrines and dogmas. A more contemporary image could be created if the church had scientific doctrines and technological dogmas. These, of course, would be continuously updated.

1a.   We find that not enough money is spent on advertising and the study of marketing techniques. We would suggest that it is not a good public relations exercise to consider people as 'sinners'.

1b.   The division of people into 'saints and sinners' or even 'Christian and non-Christian' is elitist and out of touch with modern thinking.

1c.   We suspect that to suggest people need forgiveness or God is counter-productive, leading to feelings of inadequacy and even, in extreme cases, to old-fashioned repentance.

143

Preliminary suggestions

2.   We would suggest that the church plays down its past and its emphasis on the ancient writings. People today want new things. Good marketing has instilled the idea that 'new' means 'better' and the church must take advantage of this fact.

2a.   To avoid offending the theological Luddites we would suggest that the old traditions and doctrines be translated into contemporary forms. We see no reason why the Creed should not be set to pop music; this offers the added possibility of its reaching the pop charts. With imaginative creativity Calvin's *Institutes* could probably be turned into a rock opera with a catchy title such as *Tell it as it is, Johnny.* Another possibility is an edition of the Westminster Confession of Faith produced in comic strip form.

2b.   In church services we would suggest that prayer, which is not a contemporary fashion, should be replaced with periods of meditation. Much could be learned about this from the many Gurus who are now in the religious market.

2c.   The idea that the sermon should challenge the mind and disturb the heart is now out of date. We would suggest that the church should not make people think or disturb them. There are many entertaining ways of filling the gap that would be left with the abolition of the sermon.

Conclusion

We propose that a committee be formed to work out the above observations and suggestions into a detailed programme.

We propose that the resultant scheme should be called 'Operation Ichabod'.

10
Church—I believe in the church

I believe, in the words of the Creed, that the church is holy and universal. Indeed when I go to the basis of the Creed, Scripture itself, I find it humbling and challenging to read what the New Testament has to say about the church. It is the body of Christ; the bride of Christ; a holy people, chosen, elect, called from out of all the earth to show forth the praises of the Lord till He comes. Rather than a select few called to withdraw from the world, they are to confront the world, a mighty army against which the very gates of hell will not be able to prevail. But above all, it is the church of Jesus Christ, as He said, 'I will build *my* church...'

Such words warm the heart and stir the imagination, calling out praise and glory to the King and Head of the church. Yet looking around what do I find? The church apparently weak and fragmented, unsure of its mission, uncertain of its message, confused as to its role, and even the rosiest of spectacles cannot hide the fact that there is something wrong somewhere.

So if I assert that there is a crisis in the church I am not expressing some newly-minted truth but using what is now a well-worn cliché. I must confess that this crisis does not surprise me; when it is considered how much of the Christian faith has been discarded in the development of modern theology it seems little short of a miracle that the church has survived. If the God of the church is a philosophical concept rather than a loving heavenly Father, and Jesus Christ, King and Head of the church, is merely a man who lived long ago and far away, then the church can only be a human institution. So it becomes 'our' church.

Many teachers seem to encourage us to think of the church of Jesus Christ as our church; we have the right, and responsibility, of deciding how it is to be organized, what it should say and how it should act. It would appear that it should be an expression of a consensus, what is not popular should be avoided and everything should be done in accordance with the will of the majority. All this, rather than resolving the crisis, only adds to the confusion.

A company of believers?

It seems to me that the church in our age is an uneasy alliance of every possible shade of opinion from old-fashioned, unthinking fundamentalism to radical liberalism which questions every doctrine and is prepared to discard every dogma. Those in authority try to lead from the centre and find themselves in an impossible position. There can be no advance if an army is marching in different directions at the same time.

As I see it, the problem is that, even in the realm of theology and philosophy, we are taught that all views and opinions should be treated as having equal validity. The idea that some people may be wrong, or that there is such a thing as heresy, is greeted with emotional abhorrence. In all things, I have been told, we must be broadminded, tolerant, loving, kind and never dogmatic, so we must let people believe what they like. Tolerance is the great virtue for now 'the greatest of these' is tolerance.

This means that the church of today is no longer a collection of believers who know what they believe, are united in that belief, and are prepared to confess and proclaim it. Apparently you can believe what you like and still claim to belong to the body of believers. Admittedly the situation is even further complicated by the fact that no matter how outrageous the belief or how unbiblically wild the creed, there is always some theologian, bishop, or intellectual Christian ready and willing to defend it. There are many claiming the liberty of conscience to remain within the Christian church while denying all the basic Christian doctrines.

So in the church, the company of believers, there are those who do not believe, in any sensible or meaningful way, what the church has believed and taught for centuries and what the Bible proclaims. They do not believe in creation, the Fall, miracles, virgin birth, Incarnation, substitutionary death, resurrection, judgement, heaven and hell, the second coming of the Lord; apparently many of them do not even believe in the church as being of divine origin.

I am fully aware that the sensitive noses of some will be twitching as they catch the scent of a call for a heresy hunt. They will suspect me of calling for the faggots to light afresh the fires of a new religious persecution. Probably only those who know me best will accept that I am actually a compassionate and tolerant sort of fellow who has no desire to see anyone banned or burned. But I must confess a real uneasiness at this blanket tolerance which assumes that those who do not believe the doctrines of the church should continue to be members and leaders of the church. This has come about because rather than tolerance being seen as a virtue, it has been treated as an absolute.

Perhaps the situation today is illustrated best by a parable written over two centuries ago. The German, Gotthold Lessing, wrote a short story about an ancient ring which had magical powers, giving its owner the gift of being loved by both God and man. The ring was handed down from father to son for many generations. Eventually it came into the possession of a man who had three sons whom he loved dearly. As he grew older the problem, to which son he should give the ring, troubled him greatly, since he loved them all equally. After wrestling with the problem for many years he came up with the solution. He had replicas made of the ring so that when he died each of the sons would receive a ring and none of them would know which was the genuine one; each one of them could claim to have the original and genuine ring.

Lessing, in this parable, was actually writing about religion, seeking to argue that the original cannot be traced and, as each one thinks he has the genuine one the question of the true ring does not matter. In Lessing's view, the three sons of the parable were Judaism, Christianity and Islam.

A correct interpretation of the parable for the twentieth century would require a multiplicity of rings. Every possible position and belief is equally valid and true and it does not matter who has the genuine article; as long as people think they have the real faith then that will not only help them to be loved by God and men, but will give them assurance and hope. The important thing is to hold on to our own ring and treat every other ring as being equally genuine. Tolerance is an absolute.

'We must be tolerant,' the words have often echoed in my ears and danced before my wondering eyes on the printed page. Tolerance, I am assured, is the handmaid of love. Yet, perhaps it is the simplicity of my approach, but I cannot see such an approach as being Christian or truthful; indeed it is not even love. So questions swell in my mind and problems multiply. Is it really love to allow a man to believe what we think is a lie? Is it really kindness and love to let someone walk along a dangerous path? Is it truly an expression of loving kindness to see people dedicating themselves to destructive idols and say nothing and do nothing to dissaude them? Can I say I truly love my neighbour and yet not trouble about what he either believes or does? Is tolerance really an absolute? I suspect that the comfortable middle class who lived in the bungalows around the concentration camps of Nazi Germany were tolerant. Tolerance, rather than a virtue, can be sin.

But, in spite of the suspicions I may be creating, I am not calling for an intolerant church; there is always the need for grace, sympathy and compassion and even the truth must always be spoken in love. I long to see a truly believing church, knowing what it believes and not being ashamed of its confession. After all, in spite of current theories to the contrary, belief is more important than doubt. We have absolutely no authority to say that there is more joy in heaven over one saint who doubts than the ninety and nine who dare to believe.

I suspect that if the church in our age knew what it believed and held to the beliefs as revealed in Scripture, then there would really be little need for 'heresy' trials or putting out of unbelievers. Those who did not believe would hesitate to join and, if they were members, would be so uncomfortable that they would willingly leave of their own accord. Of course there would still be differences; in a fallen world there are varying interpretations of some facets of the Christian life, but, as all the creeds and confessions make plain, there should be total acceptance of the substance of the faith which was once delivered to men.

In the new pluralism, which is a contemporary word for old-fashioned intellectual anarchy, the church is confused and uncertain. With the whole ethics of liberalism, in its many guises, dominating the Christian church, it is not surprising that many are silent when it comes to speak about their faith. The average man in the pew has either retreated into a silent, simple fundamentalism or sees Christianity as a non-rational part of life concerned with personal behaviour and Christian values. There can be little doubt that many in the church are extremely vague as to what they actually believe and are content, and perhaps taught to be content, with leaving doctrines, dogmas and theology in the hands of the experts.

Nevertheless, in spite of the climate of theological doubt, I suspect that there are many secret believers even in the most liberal of churches. Perhaps because of the way they have been brought up and other early influences, they still hold to a vague fundamentalism believing the Bible to be true. When faced with sermons and learned arguments showing the claims of modern theology, these simple people probably keep quiet, feeling almost ashamed that they find the arguments so unconvincing and silly. When everyone is cheering the emperor with his 'intellectual' gear, it is hard to cry out that he is really naked.

Perhaps I will be accused of making wild generalizations, but can anyone doubt that the flock of God seems confused and bewildered today, that they are unsure of their beliefs and uncertain why they should hold them? There is something wrong somewhere when those who do believe appear to be ashamed of their beliefs and are almost compelled to remain quiet.

The only answer is a believing church. The early church came into being throughout the Roman Empire because the apostles travelled proclaiming and affirming the truth of the gospel; many heard and believed. It is difficult to hear and believe when you are presented with arguments, doubts and philosophical speculation, and then expected to make your response. Yet I suspect that is what is happening in so many areas of the church's life today. It seems to be in danger of being treated as a debating society where every possible viewpoint is considered to be equally true, and belief and unbelief are expected to dwell happily in the house of tolerance for ever. Yet, it was the Lord who posed the question: 'Can a house divided against itself stand?'

Not of the world

The church is the people of God called to serve Him and they have been called out of the world. They are in the world, not of the world. Indeed they are to be separate and not to conform to the world in the way they think, analyse, speak or act.

Of course, there is, and probably always has been, a considerable confusion as to what is meant by the 'world'. My understanding is quite simple. The 'world' from which we are called is not the physical creation. God made the world and saw that it was good and, although it has been marred by sin, the promise of redemption will be fulfilled in the created order; all things will be made new. As I understand Scripture the 'world' from which we are to be separate is the 'kingdom of darkness', the world system which is under the rule of Satan. It is the world which refuses to recognize the sovereignty of God or the lordship of Christ. It is the world-view which takes as its focal point a man-centred view, reflecting the values, assumptions, theories and philosophies of the human mind apart from God.

I must confess an uncomfortable feeling that, rather than being separate from the world, the church at times seems scarcely indistinguishable from it. Often it is hard to see the basic difference between the godless culture and the Christian church in many areas of thought and action. Just as humanistic philosophy seems to dominate modern theology, so contemporary theories of economics and sociology influence the work and witness of the church.

Sometimes I have the nightmare that the church is really an economic institution whose main calling in the world is to raise money. I am not an incurable romantic who imagines that money, like the manna of old, will drop from heaven as we need it, but I am a Christian who has faith in God. So it troubles me that so often the church seems to be presenting a God who is a pauper — a God who needs jumble sales, sales of work, coffee mornings, endless appeals and emotive begging to carry on His work. I cannot be the only one who finds it hard to worship, or even respect, a God who depends upon the sale of old junk to carry on His work on earth. The psalmist saw his God as owning the cattle upon a thousand hills — now it often appears that the church sees Him as a God who needs every penny that can be prised out of unwilling pockets.

It is not only fund-raising which seems to take place without reference to God; often it is worldly standards that are used in measuring the effectiveness of the church. Success and failure are judged according to the standards of the age, and in the age of the mass man it is numbers that are important. So there is an obsession with numbers and, in accordance with the laws of current economics, a desire for big churches and big congregations. Jesus may have said that where two or three are gathered together in His name there He is in the midst, but now we know that such a proposition is not economically viable and Smith and Keynes are obeyed rather than Jesus.

Then there are the efforts of the church to be relevant. In my simplicity I believe that if the message of God is proclaimed then it is relevant for all men in all ages; God's Word cannot be out of date. But the way the word 'relevance' is treated today causes me concern. It does seem one of the key words in modern theology and a banner waved in the face of those who would hold to the old revealed doctrines which the church has held for centuries. I have been assured that we must be relevant and 'with it'. This usually means that we must be more existential than the existentialists, more sceptical than the sceptics, more pragmatic than the pragmatists, and more popular than the pop merchants. So there are endless efforts to show how relevant the church can be. There are rock groups, drama groups, pop concerts and pop services and all the tricks and gimmicks of modern life to show how truly relevant the church can be. I must confess that I have witnessed some of these attempts by the church to be 'with it' and have been confirmed in my view that we would be better 'without it'.

'We must move with the times' may be a suitable slogan for the evolutionists or the Marxists who believe the flow of history is taking them to the Communist paradise where the state will wither away, but is it a commandment for the church? Why must we move with the times? If, as seems to be the case in our post-Christian culture, the times are moving away from God then what must the Christian church do? To ask the question is to know the answer.

More often than not this attempt to be 'relevant' is aimed at the younger generation. The contemporary culture has proclaimed this to be the age of youth and the church would appear to have accepted blindly this coronation of the young. There was a time when wisdom was supposed to reside in the mature, and knowledge in those with long experience; now it has all changed and it is the young who must be treated as being authoritative. All opinions and activities must be judged on their appeal to the younger generation. They are hailed as the shining examples of relevance, concern, compassion and commitment; like most generalizations I suspect this is more a myth than a fact.

The youth cult in our society has come through many factors: the decline of the family and the Christian culture; affluence and the mass media creating a pop culture which encourages young people to think of themselves as different creatures. So they developed their own music, dress, hair styles and language, all to emphasize their own identity and alienate their parents. These parents, unable to understand their own children, tried to take comfort from the thought that, rather than neglecting their children, they were giving them a freedom and liberty they had never known themselves. What really happened was that these children were sacrificed to a new Moloch who devoured by manipulation, exploitation and dehumanization. The young were thrown to the pop merchants whose sole concern was profit and who were prepared to sell records, groups, clothes, posters, heroes, sex, drugs — all in the name of a new revolutionary and illusionary freedom.

What has been the church's answer to this alienation and manipulation? Rather than seeking to heal the breach between the young and old, it has apparently accepted the situation as being normative. 'Crabbed age and youth cannot live together,' wrote Shakespeare and this is treated as inerrant truth. Though I can appreciate the works of Shakespeare I do not accept without question every word he wrote, and although I have learned much from the cultural philosophers of the twentieth century I recognize them as men who can be wrong. Only the Word of God is complete and absolute truth. So I see the young Joshua and the old Moses, and the elder Paul with his young friend Timothy, as denying the generation gap and the whole concept of the youth cult.

The church of God should be, as Scripture asserts, part of the family of God on earth. In a family each member is important and all have something to contribute to the unity and diversity of the family unit. The youth cult and the blind acceptance of the current emphasis must create tensions within any family and must certainly lead to unnecessary divisions within the church as the family of God. What is needed is a healing force in the culture, the church working towards uniting the generations, rather than perpetuating the breaking up of humanity into age groups and categories. Should not the church be uniting the young and old, the weak and the strong, the innocent and the experienced, so that together they can worship and serve God for the joy and enrichment of all? Each generation has a part to play, supporting, encouraging and complementing one another; apartheid, whether racial or in ages, is wrong.

The church is not of the world, not called to follow the fashions, theories, loyalties, myths, ideological or cultural systems of the present age. The wisdom of men is foolishness to God and the church is called to obey God rather than men. So as members of the church we should never be ashamed of being different, or not conforming to the thinking of this world.

But the church is not called simply to retreat into a monastic sphere where, untroubled by conflict and challenge, she may serve God in praise and prayer. It is the church of Jesus Christ and there is the assurance that the gates of hell shall not prevail against it. It was meant to confront, not conform to, the world.

Confronting the world

The church is called to go into all the world, preaching and teaching the things of God and the gospel of Jesus Christ. It is not meant to be a social club existing for the enjoyment and benefit of its members. Yet, with the loss of sound doctrine, there is the temptation, to which many have succumbed, of seeing the church as a social organization where people of like mind and interests can enjoy being together.

All men and women, and Christians are no exceptions, have a need for social life. God made us to be gregarious creatures who enjoy being with one another, rejoicing in our common humanity in talking, singing and even laughing together. So I would hesitate to condemn any local church which provided the opportunity for members to meet and share their common humanity in activities and fellowship. The very fact that it is Christians who enjoy these things should deepen the fellowship and enrich the experience. Social activities, informal meetings and laughter are not wrong, but the church is not a social club for the enjoyment of members, with a veneer of 'Christianity' to distinguish it from the 'clubs of the world'.

Among the functions of the church I would place worship, evangelism, pastoral and social concern and a prophetic ministry, and all of them are necessary if the church is truly to obey the call of the Lord and confront the world with the truth of God. Speaking for myself, I am aware of the need for teaching so that I might be equipped to be a faithful witness to my generation. The church must be a teaching body.

Perhaps it is because I am a Scot and a Presbyterian, but I do see the sermon as crucial to the teaching of the faith, the proclamation of the Word as central to worship. In case such a confession of nationality appears to be arrogance, I must admit with shame that the days are gone when it could be said, 'Scratch a Scot and you will find a theologian.' I suspect that today, with our high rate of crime and alcoholism, if you scratched a Scot you would be in danger of having your throat cut in retaliation!

The Reformers put the sermon as central and crucial to public worship. The Word had to be taught, enabling the laity to understand the faith and helping them to confront the world with the Word of God. Today the world and, apparently, the church have changed and the great preaching and preachers are gone. Increasingly the sermon is being dispensed with or relegated to a cosy little homily which sometimes seems to owe more to the positive thinking of the *Reader's Digest* than to the Word of God. I have been assured many times, by many people, that this is the age of the ten-minute sermon liberally sprinkled with illustrations and making no intellectual demands.

I have been told of a meeting where someone described as a 'wise old minister' got up and said, 'It is sermons of more than ten minutes that are emptying the churches today.' He may have been an old minister, but I confess I would not number him among the wise. Yet it is a remarkable fact that many lay people within the church go along with this 'ten minute rule', though I have never found out who formulated the rule or by what authority it is used. Of course, I have heard many arguments in its favour. I have been told that no one can concentrate for more than ten minutes. Indeed, I will never forget how, at a conference of lay preachers, one man solemnly assured me that people cannot concentrate for more than two minutes at any one given time. It was something of a shock for me to discover that this man was actually a lecturer at a college of education and I found myself wondering if he actually practised what he preached. Of course it may well be that he had perfected the two-minute lecture and I am misjudging him. Another argument presented to me was that if a man cannot say what he wants to say in ten minutes, then he should say nothing. Logically this means that as Tolstoy could not say all he wanted in ten pages then he should never have written *War and Peace*.

What confuses my simple mind in all these arguments for short, popular little homilies is the contradictory assurance, usually given by the same people, that this is an educated age. It is unthinkingly assumed that we are wiser, more intelligent, and far more knowledgeable than our forefathers. Yet they could listen to long sermons and read lengthy theological tomes; apparently they had the ability, which we have lost, of concentrating and following complex theological arguments. Perhaps ironically, I actually have a higher opinion of my contemporaries than those who would reduce them to morons only capable of two or ten-minute flashes of rationality. I actually dare to believe that people are capable of concentrating and listening when someone has something important to say.

Having something to say is the crux of the matter. So I am

not suggesting that long sermons have a virtue in themselves; length is no criterion of excellence. It is folly to suggest that important messages must be limited in length or that the Word of God must be proclaimed in a few minutes. Perhaps it is cynicism or arrogance, but I must confess that occasionally the thought has crossed my mind that those who present few words have little to say, and those who want little sermons want little teaching.

It is teaching that we who are the laity need — teaching on how to understand the Word of God for today and how to confront the world with the Christian message. We are all called to be witnesses, ready to give reasons for our hope and faith, and in our daily life we have to live out that faith and show forth that hope. It cannot be done if we are unsure, uncertain, vague and ignorant; we must know before we can speak, and must be taught before we can teach others.

In all things concerning the church I am fearfully aware that it is easy for me to sit in judgement and, like the Pharisees of old, draw my skirts of purity away and thank God I am not as other men are. But I, too, must share the blame for the sins and shortcomings of the church. I share the responsibility for the fact that the church of today is blowing a cracked, plastic bugle that cannot be heard above the cries of despair and cursings of a world that is lost and bewildered. For me to condemn the church is to condemn myself for I am among her number and am one of the people of God called to show forth His praise and serve Him among the generation of the living.

It is also easy to fall into the temptation of despairing about the church and her future, to weep for the fragmented, confused church that, confronting the world, seems to have nothing to say. But I can rejoice in the fact that it is not my church, nor is it the church of those, learned in modern theology, who would deny all its basic doctrines. It is founded on a rock. God is still sovereign, Jesus Christ is still King and Head and the Holy Spirit is still present, capable of bringing life into the valley of the dry bones of modern theology.

I like the legend of an Eastern prince who, during the early Renaissance, travelled the world seeking the one true religion. After visiting many sacred cities and shrines, he reached Rome where the medieval popes and cardinals were living in open sin and every vice was rampant. After seeing the corruption and wickedness, he announced to his astonished courtiers that he was going to become a Christian. Horrified, his courtiers pointed out the sacred places they had been to, and the holy men they had met, and compared that to the iniquity they had found in the capital of the Christians. The prince listened to their arguments but was firm in his decision, telling them, 'When I see what the leaders of this Christian faith are doing, how vile and evil they are, and find that this faith has survived for centuries, then I know that God must be there. This faith would not have lasted in the hands of such men unless God was preserving it.'

The church has survived. There have been many false prophets and teachers over the centuries and there can be no doubt they are still with us. There are still false shepherds creating havoc in the flock and letting wolves roam into the fold. But the future of the church ultimately is in the hands of the Good Shepherd and all power is in His hands.

I love the church and know that it will be triumphant, for Jesus Christ said it was 'my church and the gates of hell shall not prevail against it'. So it grieves me that today it seems to be hell that is advancing and the gates of the church that are yielding. It pains me that those who have been gifted with brilliant minds and analytical brains to be teachers and theologians of the church should use their gifts to deny His Word, overthrow the historical creeds and cast doubt on the doctrines of the faith.

I want to see the church like a mighty army, the army of God, united and strong, going forth in the power of God's Spirit, proclaiming the truth that is to be found in God's Word. I want to see her as truly the people of God, worshipping and witnessing, rejoicing in salvation and all the good gifts of our Father God. I want to see her confronting the world; advancing, not retreating; proclaiming, not apologizing; prophesying, not just debating — a church who knows what she believes, and is unashamed to stand on the Word of God which liveth and abideth for evermore.

I believe in the Bible, the inerrant, inspired Word of God. I believe in the church and from men I ask for no pity for my simplicity.

Nightmare
A psalm for modern sheep

There is no shortage of shepherds
And I shall not want for ways to go.
They make me lie down in ambiguous pastures,
Or lead me in all directions.
They stimulate my imagination,
Leading me into obscure paths for their own name's sake.
Yea, though I walk through the valley of doubt
I will hear no certainties, for they are with me,
Their words and concepts confusing me.
They prepare a table before me,
Furnished with the ideas of mine enemies,
They anoint my head with controversies,
My rationality runneth over.
Surely there is simplicity and assurance
Or must I dwell in the maze of perplexity for ever?

Epilogue
A final bleat

The bleating and butting are over and all the baaings and booings are finished. This cantankerous old sheep may have irritated many worldly-wise shepherds but he hopes above all that he may have written something to comfort those trusting sheep who, like himself, want to hold on to their simplicity. After all, he knows that there is a simplicity in Christ, the Chief Shepherd.

Now, at the end of the book, this sheep is painfully aware that what has been produced falls far short of a real confession of faith. There are many areas on which he has been silent and, often, what he has written has not been systematically argued out or developed. At times he has wandered afar after the manner of all sheep. But it is hard to see the straight and narrow path of truth when the grey mist of theological confusion hangs over everything and the thickets of modern thought are sprouting all around.

So many of the great doctrines of the faith have been ignored or mentioned without discussion. But he is aware that they, too, are under attack, not only from the wild beasts that roam a godless world, but they are in danger within the fold from wolves in shepherds' clothing. Even though he is not a theologian, he does regret leaving out great themes and doctrines such as the providence of God, God's covenant with His people, the sacraments, and the crucial battlefields of free will, the calling of God and the perseverance of the saints. He has said practically nothing about the church's mission to a lost world in evangelism and the relative merits of a spiritual gospel, social gospel, ethical gospel, political gospel, and the fifty-seven other varieties that are now on offer. He has been largely silent on prophecy, witness, prayer and praise. Although it was difficult, he resisted the temptation to discuss those Christians who, avoiding all firm declarations of faith, proudly assert that they stand in the middle of the road. Even to a sheep's brain this seems the most stupid of all places to stand. But he can only mention all these things to show that he is aware they exist and are important – even though the liberal sheepdogs think they have chased them out of existence.

Although he makes no apology for this book, he does regret the climate that has made it necessary. If his satires seem cruel perhaps he should express contrition but, truth to tell, they are not as harsh as they could be; his laughter is Byronic: 'I laugh that I might not weep.' Having read and heard from so much modern liberal theology concerning the death of simple old-fashioned Christianity he has found, like Oscar Wilde's description of the death of Little Nell, that one would have to have a heart of stone to read it without laughing.

But perhaps he should end where he began, confessing an awareness of the reaction that will follow the bleating of his wandering confession. He knows full well that some will dismiss him as a fool of a sheep, typical of the species, while others will see him as a danger to the unity of the fold in the contemporary world. In the liberal philosophy all beliefs are valid except simple belief in the Bible. So some may long to see him driven into a zoo for endangered species where he could be studied as a relic from the dead past.

To be old-fashioned, as he is painfully aware, is the really unforgivable sin of the twentieth century. He will be accused of blindly refusing to see the light of modern scholarship, science which is infallible and inerrant, philosophy which is the light of truth, psychology which is the special revelation, anthropology which is sacred history, and all the other ologies produced by the deep thought of sinful men in a godless age. But this particular sheep can make no apology for refusing to believe that the light of God's Word is wrong and that to believe it is intellectual darkness. He cannot accept that the faith of his fathers was false.

Others must judge, but he does not think he is naive. As a lamb of this century, he knows the culture and society and has seen the great movements of his age. Often, within the fold and without, he has wondered who indeed is going in the right direction — himself or his critics. Yet it was a modern poet that reminded him that in a world of refugees it will be the one advancing who seems to be running away. So this poor, simple sheep is content to move towards God and His Word rather than join the flight of modern thought away from the source of wisdom and salvation.

So he is aware that he may be dismissed as having too simplistic a view of creation, Fall and redemption. Perhaps his theology will be seen as too glib and easy for those who trust the gods of humanistic achievement and the power of secular philosophy. If this is so, he cannot find it in his heart to offer apologies for either his theology or his views.

If he is too simple, then he has this great comfort and hope: the good and great Shepherd, who gave His life for the sheep and knows them all by name, will pity the simplicity of this poor little sheep.